Common

Common Sense Discipline

Building Self-Esteem in Young Children

Stories from Life

Grace Mitchell
Lois Dewsnap

Photographs by Nancy Alexander

TelShare Publishing
Glen Burnie, Maryland

Copyright © 1995 Grace Mitchell and Lois Dewsnap
Published by TelShare Publishing Company
6473 Freedom Drive, Glen Burnie, MD 21061

Cover Design: Lightbourne Images
Text Photos: Nancy Alexander

Library of Congress Cataloging-in-Publication Data
  Mitchell, Grace L.
    Common sense discipline : building self-esteem in young
  children: stories from life / Grace Mitchell, Lois Dewsnap.
      p. cm.
    Includes bibliographical references and index.
    ISBN 0-910287-11-2 (pbk.)
    1. Discipline of children. 2. Problem children. 3. Self-esteem
  in children. I. Dewsnap, Lois F. II. Title.
  HQ770.4.M55 1995
  649'.84—dc20   95-11901
                                                                      CIP

Acknowledgments

W e would like to express our appreciation to the following people who gave generously of their time to help us gather material for this book.

Mary-Ellen Arsenault, owner, Madeline Gentile, Director, and the staff of First Steps

Diane Barter, Teacher/Parent

Debra Beyer, Director; Susan Russell, owner and staff of Neighborhood Kids

Pamela Callahan, teacher

Frank Cotter, Waltham Public Schools, School Counselor

Judy DeRoche, Owner/Director of Koala School

Karen Dewey, Lisa and Joanne, and Dr. Betsy Gibbs of Newport

Noreen Edge, Gauldin School

Marcia Galazzi, Owner, Carolyn O'Leary, and the staff of The Family Schools

Sally Goldberg, Director of Children's Science Resource Center

Hope Gordon, School Counselor

Annie Hale, Director, Children's Way

Joanne C. Holmes, Early Childhood Consultant, Child Development Services

Nan Howkins, Owner/Director, My Nursery School

Deborah Ireland, Waltham Public Schools, Principal

Ellen Kerstein, Parent

Ida Marie Kreiser, Teacher

Susan L'Aventure, Director of National Association for Parents of the Visually Impaired

Debbie Phelps, Teacher

Connie Rocha, Owner/Director, Cariño Child Care Center

Shelley Rossman, Director, Temple Emuneh

Antoinette Russell, Teacher

Pat Sanford, Owner of Tech Ed Services

Anne Stevens, Program Coordinator of Bath-Brunswick Child Care Services, and her staff

Cynthia Wallace, Owner of Children's Centre, Inc.

Brenda Wilkinson, Owner/Director of Brenda's Small World

Susan Wolf-Fordham, parent and child advocate

Terry Wydrat, Parent

Table Of Contents

Part One—
Today's Family
Patterns & Discipline

Sue Ellen
"She's been here almost two weeks, and I haven't
seen her smile once."
Divorced mother raising her child alone

Tod
"My Mom and Dad both went away. I hate living
with my grandparents!"
Grandparents raising their grandchild

Penny
"I can't read! How can I help Penny?"
Grandmother with minimal education raising her grandchild

Lenny
"You're mean! I hate you! I want to go
live somewhere else!"
Practical problems of foster parents and children

Part Two—
Inclusive Education
and Discipline

Part Three—
Mistakes Adults Make

Discipline is the slow, bit-by-bit, time consuming task of helping children see the sense in acting a certain way.

Today's society is not an easy one to live in, for parents, teachers *or* children! Adults are trying to cope with *stress*, caused by changing family structures, changing attitudes and rules, and uncertainty about their own ability to "keep their heads above water" financially. We believe that teachers in early childhood education, especially in child care centers and family home care, are at the end of a "domino" effect. Parents who are under severe stress because of problems they can't control act in ways that affect their children. No matter how hard they try to conceal their feelings, or shelter their youngsters from their own worries, it doesn't work. Children have "a kind of radar" that tells them when all is not right in their world. They, in turn, may be fearful—"What is going to happen to me?", bewildered—"Why am I being sent to stay with Grandma?" or guilty—"Did Daddy go away because I was bad?" Trying to get answers often means going to the people who are causing the problem, so the child waits till he is on neutral ground—the child care center—where all those feelings come out. This hypothesis is supported by the many teachers we have talked to who have said, "This job is so much harder than it was when I first started teaching."

In this book we will talk about divorce and stepfamilies, single parents, grandparents raising grandchildren, violence among children, multicultural misunderstandings, including children with disabilities in regular classrooms and common mistakes adults make. Using what we believe about discipline, this book offers suggestions and support to parents and teachers alike.

What is this book going to do for you?

♦ **Reach Your Heart and Mind**

A story enables people to remember what is important. The format of this book, then, relies heavily on stories, followed by our thoughts and suggestions. Because we are dealing with the problems parents and teachers face, the stories are apt to be poignant and thought-provoking, rather than humorous, but we believe they *do* reinforce the points we want to make.

We have gathered many stories. As we have traveled and met with parents and teachers, we heard many stories and anecdotes. Sometimes, they come from our own observations. We have "fleshed them out," but they all start with an actual happening.

♦ **Broaden Your Outlook and Make You Think**

As you read about the stressful situations faced by parents and teachers in today's changing society, you will see beyond the boundaries of your own world. Descriptions of children in different settings will give you insight into all children and help you understand the needs of those youngsters under your care.

♦ **Offer Positive Help**

Within the stories themselves and in the comments that follow them, you will find suggestions for techniques and strategies that you can apply to your own situations.

There are behavior problems that have been with us from the beginning of time, and are part of a child's normal pattern of growing up. The last part of this book is called "Mistakes Adults Make," and shows how many of these everyday problems can be prevented, or at least minimized.

◆ Inform and Reassure

The responsibility of raising a child with a disability has long rested on the parents alone. Now that the Americans With Disabilities Act (ADA) has mandated that these children be accepted in regular schools, including private and state supported preschools, teachers find themselves face-to-face with many problems they never expected to have.

The reaction on the part of many teachers has been a mixture of fear and anger. Fear of the unknown that lies ahead of them, anger because they are being told they have to take on tasks that weren't "in the picture" when they signed on for the job.

In Part Two we will give you more information about the Act and show you that your fears may not be necessary.

◆ Provide Discipline Techniques and Strategies

When people speak of *discipline problems*, they really mean behavior problems. They are usually thinking of children who are disruptive and aggressive—real troublemakers. They may not include children who are withdrawn, who never take part or make friends, yet this, too, is a behavior problem. The youngster who is too quiet may be compared to a fire in the forest that is smoldering along the roots of the trees, underground, unseen and unsuspected, until the day it bursts out in flames.

A child who is fearful and confused, who feels rejected, humiliated or guilty, who has low self-esteem, may withdraw or strike out. On the other hand, a child who feels loved and safe, who is supported and encouraged, is going to be happy and confident, and may not need to "act out."

Think of discipline as *education*. Teach children how to feel better about themselves by conforming to the standards set by society. Make an effort to give children the kind of support *all* human beings need. This approach may take longer, but there's a much better chance that the change will be permanent. Adults who believe *discipline* means *punishment* are going to defeat their own purpose. Anger, sarcasm and rejection *may* control the symptoms—the child's present actions—but will not cure the underlying cause.

We do not advocate permissiveness. We believe in setting limits. However, we *know*, from years of experience, that the positive approach works. We urge you to think, in every action you take, "Will this really solve the problem? Will it help Julio—or Roger—or Wendy—or Carlita—to be a happier, more self-confident, and *better-behaved* child?"

Today's Family Patterns & Discipline

I N RECENT YEARS, a new word has come to the forefront when we talk about discipline—STRESS! What causes stress?

- ◆ Patrick O'Brien has lost his job because the company he worked for has been purchased by another, larger company. He has a wife, four children, no job, no health insurance!

- ◆ Tamara West is struggling to balance the needs of her family with the demands of her career.

- ◆ Ms. Nelson is at a loss when the children in her second grade reflect the violence they see on television.

Although we have included a chapter on violence and another on cultural misunderstandings, most of the chapters in this section have to do with changing family structures, the stress they might cause and the subsequent discipline problems due, in part, to this increased stress. For the purposes of this book, we will define a family as the people living under one roof and being responsible for the children living there.

The family unit has always been a major factor in society. A few decades ago, most families consisted of a mother and father, and one or more children. Sometimes an aunt or grandparent also lived in the home. The parents set standards for their children. There was no confusion about who was in charge, no questioning whether or not one would obey. Oh, children went through various stages of rebellion, but they generally knew just how far they could go before the consequences outweighed the temporary satisfaction of getting away with something.

What are some of the major changes in today's families?

According to recent statistics, fifteen million children under age eighteen now live in *stepfamilies*. The arrangement can be fairly simple. Rosa lives with her mother and stepfather, and her birth father is not in the picture. Far more complicated is Tilda's situation. Her mother married Ray, who brought three sons to the union. Now they have a new baby. How does that make Tilda feel? And how does she feel about the time she spends with Dennis, her own father, and his wife, Ava? What signals is she picking up from all these grownups? bitterness? confusion? cooperation?

Another change is that of *both parents working outside the home*. Few households today include extended family members such as aunts and grandparents. The children are cared for at home by a paid child care worker or are in a child care arrangement outside the home. These parents are trying to meet the demands of a career *and* the demands of raising a family. Talk about stress!

We also have a growing number of *grandparents* pushed into the role of raising a second family. When the courts decide it is unsafe for children to live with their parents, grandparents often step into the role of parents. Teen pregnancy, when the father is unknown or has refused to accept responsibility, and the mother is emotionally and financially unready to be a parent is another situation when grandparents become parents.

The growing exposure of young children to *violence* is affecting family life in a different way. Children view violent television programs filled with fist fights and beatings, shootings, exploding cars and buildings. Sometimes it is the police officer, the "good guy," who is committing the violent acts. In addition, many children witness violent acts in their everyday lives. The message is that violence is the way to solve problems. When the children who have learned this lesson express anger or frustration by hitting or swearing at their parents, they are often punished with a spanking or worse—more violence.

Also included in this section is an example of what can happen when a teacher moves into a community where the *culture* is very different from his or her own background.

All these changes create stress and challenging discipline situations for parents and teachers.

Communication between parents and teachers is an absolute must. Ms. Bertini will be more ready to "go the extra mile" with Jordan's disruptive behavior if she knows what is causing him to strike out at the world. At the same time, Jordan's parents have a right to assume that anything they tell Ms. Bertini will be held in strictest confidence. Also, the parents may believe that once their son is in school everything will be fine. Unless the teacher tells them what is happening, they can never work together to help Jordan work out his problems.

In the midst of all of these challenges and stress, we recognize and applaud the parents, stepparents, working parents, single parents, grandparents and teachers who are working hard to give children the love and support they need to live healthy, happy lives.

1

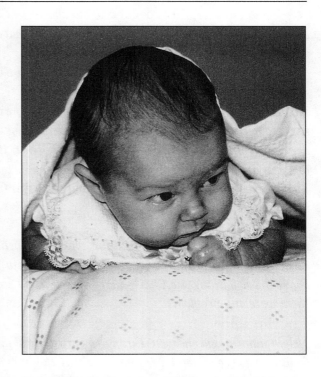

"She's been here almost two weeks, and I haven't seen her smile once."

"Oh, sweetheart, what is it?" crooned infant care giver Florence Evans to the baby she was cuddling in her arms. "Why are you always so solemn? Why don't you ever look happy?"

Just then Ms. Gagnon, the director, walked into the room. "Oh, I'm so glad you came in!" exclaimed Florence. "I've been wanting to talk to you about Sue Ellen. I'm really worried about her."

"What's wrong?" asked the child care director. "Actually, she's the reason I'm here. I didn't know there was a problem, but usually when a new child enters

---

the program I keep an eye on things for awhile. I haven't heard any crying, though."

"No," said Florence, "she doesn't cry, but she doesn't laugh either. She doesn't even smile. She's been here almost two weeks, and I haven't seen her smile once."

"Not even when her mother comes for her?" asked Ms. Gagnon in surprise.

No, not even then, and since I've been watching more closely, I've realized that her mother never smiles, either. She always looks sad and tired—really depressed. But it's Sue Ellen I'm concerned about. It just isn't natural for a one year old not to smile at all, and one thing you've taught me in the five years I've been working here is that when a child strays far from typical developmental stages, there's trouble ahead."

Ms. Gagnon nodded. "You're quite right. I haven't said anything before because it might not have been necessary, but now you need to know more about the situation. Sue Ellen's mom agreed that I could tell you about this if there were any problems.

"Eight months ago she went through a very painful divorce. She had difficulty finding a job, and isn't very happy about the one she has. She had several unsatisfactory baby sitters before she came to us, and everything is just weighing her down. She looks depressed because she is depressed. I don't want to add to her problems by telling her about Sue Ellen until we come up with something specific to suggest, so we'll think about this and then call her in here. However, we will not let this go longer than one or two days."

Preventive discipline

Nowadays we hear a lot about "preventive medicine." You might call this "preventive discipline." Both Ms. Gagnon and Florence were conscious of the fact that a child who doesn't progress along the typical stages of child development is not going to have a strong "I Am," or sense of self-esteem. Without that "I Am," there *will* be trouble. A good teacher notices when a child is "off track," and works to straighten out problems before more serious ones develop.

Language develops faster in babies when parents and other care givers talk to them. Responding to the infant's gurgles and grunts with a similar sound is the groundwork for communication.

Children of all ages are very sensitive to the feelings of the adults who care for them. Florence and Ms. Gagnon felt that Sue Ellen might well be responding to the feeling of sadness she sensed in her mother. Added to that, Florence had been so worried about this solemn child, that she wasn't her usual, cheerful self when she was with Sue Ellen.

School and home cooperating towards a common goal

Florence and Mrs. Gagnon decided that every adult in the center who had any contact with Sue Ellen would present a smiling face and cheerful tone of voice. The other, and most important, part of their plan was to ask Mrs. Phillips to make a conscious effort to smile at her daughter, no matter how she felt. Mrs. Phillips loved her baby and wanted the best for her. She just hadn't realized how her own attitude was affecting Sue Ellen. Once she understood, she did make the effort, and within a few weeks there was a remarkable difference. Sue Ellen became a happier baby, and her mother confessed that her own spirits lifted in the process.

The steps of good communication

The steps taken by the director and teacher in this chapter bear repeating.

Recognize the problem. It was Florence, the teacher, who first recognized that Sue Ellen never smiled. If a parent does not notice a problem, often the teacher who spends the most time with the child will be the one to notice it.

Communicate with the director. If Mrs. Gagnon hadn't come in when she did, Florence would have gone to her. In a preschool, often it is the director who contacts the parents.

Decide on a goal and a plan. The goal in this case was to help Sue Ellen become a happy baby. The plan was to involve other staff members and the mother in providing an atmosphere in which this baby could be happy.

Communicate the goal to all staff. Depending on the size of the staff and the complexity of the problem, this could be done in a short meeting during nap time, or in a more lengthy staff meeting after regular school hours.

Communicate with parent(s). To resolve a problem effectively, parent(s) and teachers must communicate and cooperate.

2

Tod

"My mom and dad both went away. I hate living with my grand-parents!"

Mrs. Rodriguez frowned as she looked through the pile of papers on her desk. "Tod Chapell, you haven't turned in your paper yet," she said. "Please bring it up now."

The slim, dark-haired boy shrugged. "I didn't do it," he announced flatly. "That stuff is dumb. Who wants to write about a stupid television program about polar bears? I didn't even bother to watch it."

"He couldn't watch it," jeered another boy. "His grammy wouldn't let him. He has to go to bed at eight o'clock, like my little sister."

"Oh, no!" thought Mrs. Rodriguez, and started to her feet, but Tod was too fast for her. In an instant he had dashed across the room and attacked Frank with a fury that was startling to see in a seven year old boy. Both boys were yelling, using language that made the teacher shudder. The other children were watching in fascination, some out of their seats shouting encouragement, others obviously frightened.

Quickly, Mrs. Rodriguez came up behind Tod and managed to pull him away from Frank. With an effort, she held him, her arms around him, holding his arms at his sides.

"All of you sit down at once and take out your reading books," she announced in tones that brooked no argument. "Frank, go to your seat. I'll talk to you later."

As things settled down, she moved to one side, still holding Tod. She could feel his rigid body trembling. Quietly, she started murmuring to him. "It's all over, Tod. Calm down. Take a deep breath. Stand quietly. It's over." Gradually, she felt his body relax. When the stiffness had gone and the trembling had stopped, she asked softly, so only he could hear, "Are you all right now? If I let you go, will you go quietly to your desk?" He nodded, she let go, and he went back to his place.

She said no more about the missing paper then, but when the children lined up for dismissal, she spoke directly to him. "Tod, please stay for a minute."

You have a violent temper. When all the others had left, she went over and sat down next to him. "Tod, we need to talk," she said. "Can you stay now, or would you rather come in early in the morning?"

Again he shrugged. "I'll stay," he muttered.

"Tod, have you ever seen a child who was blind, or someone whose legs were paralyzed, who had to sit in a wheelchair?" she asked. He nodded.

"Well, that is called a disability, and Tod, you have a disability. You have a violent temper. If you don't do something about it, someday you may hurt someone very badly.

"Whaddaya mean?" asked Tod uncertainly.

"You are a smart boy—smart enough to be the boss of your own body. Fighting never solves anything; it just gets you into trouble. You can learn to use your brains, not your fists. You can control your temper."

"Well, he made me so mad!" flared the child. "He shouldn'ta said what he did."

How to channel anger

"You're right," agreed the teacher, "and I'll talk to him later. Right now I want to give you some ideas on how to deal with that temper. I'm going to bring in some rags tomorrow, and put them in my closet. When you start to see red, to get so mad you have to do something, take some rags out in the hall and tear them up. Another thing—and I do this sometimes when I am mad—is simply taking deep breaths. Breathe in as much air as you can, then let it out slowly, while you count to ten. Pretend that when you breathe in you are filling up a balloon, and when you breathe out the air is going out of the balloon. Do this six or seven times, and you'll feel yourself calming down. Will you try these things?"

"Yeah, I guess so," muttered the boy.

"Now, tell me why you got so mad. Do you live with your grandmother?"

"Yeah, and my grandfather. And I hate living with them. They're mean! I can't do anything the other kids do. I can't go to the park and play ball. I have to wear a shirt every day, not a T-shirt like the other kids. They make me go to bed early, and I can't watch TV except on Saturday. I have to do dishes and make my bed and take out the trash. None of the other kids have to do all those things. And Gram and Gramps don't like the way I talk. They're always yelling at me. They don't want me and I don't want them, but my parents went away and dumped me on them."

Mrs. Rodriguez was silent for a moment, trying to swallow the lump in her throat. Finally, with a smile, she said, "All right, Tod, you can go now. I don't want you to be late getting home."

"Are you going to tell them what I did?" he demanded.

"I'll have to talk to them," she said, "but I'll try not to say anything that will make them mad at you."

When Tod left, she went to the principal, told him what had happened, and that she would like to have a conference with the grandparents. "Do you want to be there?" she asked.

"I think it might be better if you handled it as you would any conference," he said thoughtfully. "If I am there, it may alarm them—put them on the defensive. Is there any other way I can help?"

"Yes, would you call them tomorrow after Tod has left for school and ask them to come in at 12:30? That is my lunch hour."

"You don't have to give up your lunch hour," Mr. Santini said firmly. "I'll make it at 1:30 and send in someone to cover your room."

Communicating with the grandparents

"Thank you for coming Mrs. Chapell, Mr. Chapell," said Mrs. Rodriguez. "Please sit down. I want to talk with you about Tod."

"What's that damn kid done now?" *exploded the man facing her. (She judged him to be in his late sixties, his wife a little younger.) "He's been nothing but trouble ever since he came to live with us."*

"Please, Thomas, he's our grandchild, our son's child, our own blood," his wife protested nervously.

"Yeah, well he's her blood, too, and that's bad blood. Our son never acted like Tod."

"How does Tod act at home?" asked the teacher.

"He's lazy, doesn't think he should have to do any work around the house, not even keep his own room clean. He talks back when I tell him to do something, he swears—I never heard such language from a kid! He hangs around with a bunch of hoodlums, and if we'd let him, he'd go to school dressed like a bum."

"Thomas, you're talking about him like he was sixteen," said his wife. "He's only a child." Turning to Mrs. Rodriguez, she said earnestly, "We're just too old to be doing this. Our Bill was 28 when he got married. Francie was just 20. She was a pretty little thing, but she was like a child. She never had to raise a finger at home, and she didn't know how to take care of a house and a kid. Bill would get mad when he came home and the house was a mess and the kid was dirty. It got so they were fighting more and more, and they were always yelling at each other. Then the company where Bill worked closed and he lost his job, and one day last year, Francie just packed up her things and walked out. Bill moved in with us, and then he got a chance at a job in another state. He left Tod with us—what else could he do?"

"It must be very hard," said the teacher sympathetically.

"Everything is so different these days!" *exclaimed Mrs. Chapell. "Tod wants to go to school in jeans and a T-shirt. When Bill was little, boys wore pants and shirts to school, and changed to jeans when they came home. I taught him to keep his room clean and help around the house. We never swore in front of him, and if he picked up a bad word outside and used it, we made sure he never used it again. And he never talked back. I guess that bothers me most of all."*

"What bothers me is that Tod seems to think we owe him something," said Mr. Chapell. "Bill sends some money now and then, but it's costing us plenty to have him here. We don't have a lot of money saved, but when I retired two years ago, we thought we could take it easy, maybe travel a bit, maybe move to Florida, away from the snow and cold. Now we're stuck raising another kid, and he isn't even grateful. He acts like he hates us."

Providing helpful suggestions

Family Counseling Service. *Mrs. Rodriguez took a deep breath. "The school system has a Family Counseling Service, and I would urge you to make an appointment. They could help you to understand Tod better and work out your difficulties. For my part, I wanted to talk to you about his work and his behavior in school. I do want to say a couple of things. First, Tod thinks you hate him, that you don't want him. That's a hard thing for a child to live with, and it may well be why he seems to be so angry in school. He has a quick temper, and is ready to fight anytime. I had a talk with him yesterday about his temper, which I want to tell you about."*

She explained to them what she had said to Tod, and the suggestions she had made. "I never thought of temper that way," said Tod's grandmother.

Tod is only a little boy. *"The other thing is what you said, Mrs. Chapell. Tod is only a little boy. He doesn't quite dare show his feelings to you, so he comes to school and swaggers and talks back and refuses to do his work. The other children tease him because he doesn't dress the way they do, or have as much freedom. I think he is trying to show them that he can act the way he wants to."*

"Well, what are you suggesting?" asked Mr. Chapell irritably. "If you're telling us we should let him have his own way all the time, forget it."

Get to know other parents. *"No, of course not," said the teacher. "But there are a couple of things you might do. For one thing, come to the PTA meetings. It would give you a chance to know some of the parents of the other children, and to learn some of the ways things are different today.*

Talk and listen. *"The other thing is to talk to Tod and listen to him. Explain the rules you have laid down, and listen to his side. Perhaps you will see ways that you can change, ways that will make him feel better but won't go against your basic principles. I ask you not to scold or punish him because of anything I have told you. You see, I don't think he really wants to be bad, he just doesn't quite know how to cope with his true unhappiness."*

"We'll try," promised Mrs. Chapell, rising to go. "We'll think about all you said. Anyway, thanks for trying to help Tod."

3

"I can't read! How can I help Penny?"

Agnes Boulet sat down nervously across from Fern Ellis, her granddaughter's teacher and Sylvia Fredette, the school counselor. "I sure hope this is important," she blustered. "I had to take off work to come here. I can't afford to lose pay—I hardly make ends meet as it is. What's Penny done that's so bad I had to come see you?"

Miss Ellis shook her head. "Penny hasn't done anything bad," she reassured the other woman. "It's just that she needs help, and I thought between us we could find a way to give her that help."

"What kind of help?" asked Mrs. Boulet, still suspicious. "You sure she isn't in trouble?"

"Penny is falling behind in her schoolwork," Fern said simply. "I'm sorry to say this, but Penny doesn't do her homework, she has failed a number of tests, and if she doesn't improve, we'll have to keep her in third grade for another year. Her IQ tests show that she is capable of learning, but that Penny has a lot of trouble with reading, which makes it hard for her to do any of her work, whether it's social studies, science, language arts, or even math—because math isn't just numbers. I have taken certain steps to help her. For one thing, she is on the list to work with our volunteer tutor, but that only happens once a week. Another thing I have done is assign a peer tutor to Penny..."

"What's that—a peer tutor?" interrupted Mrs. Boulet.

"A peer tutor is another student, someone her own age who is good in reading. In this case, it's Adele Cormier. Twice a week we end the day with half an hour of open time, when the children can choose to work on a special project, something they really like to do. It might be painting, or a science experiment, or working on a play. Adele chooses to be a tutor."

"That's pretty nice of her," said Mrs. Boulet slowly. "She must be a good kid."

"She is," agreed Fern. "However, the point is that with a little extra help, Penny does manage. If you could help her at home each night, she could probably keep up."

The other woman bristled. "When am I supposed to do that?" she demanded. "I'm a chambermaid at the Sleepwell Motel. All day I make beds and clean rooms. When I get home at night, I'm too tired to do anything but get us something to eat. On my day off, I clean our place and do the laundry and stuff like that. Penny's eight years old, she could do the work if she wanted to. She's just lazy, she doesn't try."

"Oh, I don't think Penny is lazy, I think she is discouraged," responded Miss Ellis. "When a child can't read well, it's frustrating. She needs you to help her, and she needs to know you think she can do it."

"I can't read myself!" "Well, she won't get help from me," yelled the other woman angrily, jumping to her feet. "How can I help her when I can't read myself!" She looked ready to bolt from the room.

Talking about the problem

Fern Ellis, taken aback by the sudden outburst, was at a loss for words. Sylvia Fredette, the school counselor, came around her desk quickly, and held out her hand. "Mrs. Boulet, I'm the one who called and asked you to come in. We do appreciate your taking time off work to come, and we're sorry if we have upset you. Please sit down, and let's start over. It says in Penny's folder that you are her grandmother and her legal guardian. Can you tell us about that?"

Agnes sat down, her anger fading. "I never finished high school," she said. "I hated school—everything was too hard. And then this boy got me pregnant. Back then, you had to leave school if you got pregnant. So I had Marilyn when I was just sixteen. Doug and I got married, but he didn't really want to, you know? He got a job, and we tried to make a go of it, but it didn't last. When Marilyn was three, he took off. He sent me money for a couple of years, but when she started going to school he stopped. I did whatever I could find, cleaning houses, waiting on tables, anything that paid a couple of bucks."

She stopped, and Sylvia murmured sympathetically, "It must have been very hard."

"I wasn't going to let them send her to some foster home." "Yeah, well, you do what you gotta do, you know? Anyway, Marilyn did better than I did in school, and I thought things were going to be okay, but when she was sixteen, *she did the same dumb thing I did—got pregnant, and had Penny. Only she didn't even try to marry the guy, she just took the baby and moved in with him. I tried to keep in touch, but she never wanted me to go see her. Then one day a lady came to see me, a social worker, you know, and told me they had taken the baby away from Marilyn because she and that guy were on drugs. They weren't taking care of Penny, she wasn't getting enough food, and the neighbors said they were hitting her—they heard the kid screaming and called the police. So I had to go to court, and a judge said they would have to send Penny to a foster home unless I would take her. Well, this was my grandkid they were talking about. I wasn't going to let them send her to some foster home. So I took her."*

She took a deep breath, then went on. "She was really a good baby, I loved her—I still do. I got a night job cleaning offices, and I had to leave the kid alone, but my neighbor was real good, she looked in on her, and went over if she heard her crying. But I never got much sleep, because I had to take care of Penny in the daytime, so when she got in school, I found this job where I could work days. I can keep her fed and buy her clothes, but I sure can't help her with school work."

Supporting the parent's efforts. *"Mrs. Boulet, you're wonderful! I do admire you!" said Sylvia sincerely. "It took a lot of courage, and you have done a good job with Penny. It shows—she is really a nice little girl—everyone likes her." Turning to Penny's teacher, Mrs. Fredette continued, "Miss Ellis, will you explain what happens next?"*

Explaining the school's plan

Fern leaned forward. "I understand now why you didn't come to Parents' Night or answer my notes, Mrs. Boulet. In this school system, before I can get the help of a reading specialist for Penny, there are certain steps to be taken. I must work within the classroom to give Penny extra help; you and I must meet

---

twice so I can explain what we have done; and then we set up a child study team. Mrs. Fredette and I would be part of that team. If the people on the team decide it is justified, they can recommend an evaluation be done to pinpoint what her specific problems are. Depending on the test results, she might qualify for additional services.

"I will work out a plan to give Penny additional help." *"Why don't we do this? I will work out a plan to give Penny additional help. Some of this might mean keeping her half an hour after the regular school day, if you don't object. In a month we will meet again. Perhaps we could set a time first thing in the morning, or late afternoon, so you wouldn't have to take off as much time from work. I really think we might be able to solve this problem, but it is essential that we keep in touch, if only by phone. Will you do that?"*

"Yeah, I'll manage that," said Agnes slowly. "I didn't realize how important it was for me to come in. Penny can stay after school, all right. There's nothing she has to hurry home for."

Grandparents raising grandchildren

Sylvia spoke up again. "I know Miss Ellis has to get back to her work, but could you give us just a few more minutes? You know, there are a lot of women like you, raising their grandchildren. Did you know there was an association called 'Grandparents Raising Grandchildren' that was started just to help?"

"No, I never heard of that," said Mrs. Boulet.

"Well, as it happens, there is a chapter in this city. If your neighbor would look after Penny one night a week, I think you would find it very helpful to go to the meetings. If you are interested, I'll have someone call you and tell you more about it. It doesn't cost anything, and if you try it and it doesn't help, you don't have to go back."

The other woman looked doubtful. "Well," she said hesitantly, "I guess it's all right for someone to call, but I'm not promising to go."

"Fair enough," said Sylvia briskly. "Thank you again for coming in, and try not to worry. Miss Ellis is going to do all she can to help Penny."

The school guidance counselor who told us this story assured us that it was not at all unusual. She had met with many grandparents who were having to raise another generation just when they thought that job was behind them. The difficulties this brings are many and varied.

For grandparents, child rearing is a strain. Agnes Boulet was doing it alone. Being a single parent is hard enough at any age, but an older parent finds it a physical strain, as well as an emotional one.

Giving up a dream of extra money and free time. Some couples, as in the last chapter, have been looking forward to retirement as a time to relax and have a little fun. Then, they have to give up that dream. The money they had saved, the free time they expected to have, are eaten up by the responsibilities of this new child in their lives.

Feeling helpless. It isn't always a case of not wanting to take on the care of a grandchild—sometimes it's more a feeling of helplessness. "I'm just too old for this," is a common protest. "I don't have the energy to take care of young children."

A school counselor's first responsibility is to the child. Penny had a problem. The teacher followed the usual procedure of trying to reach the person named as legal guardian. When she got no response, she went to Mrs. Fredette for help. Miss Ellis needed to talk to Penny's grandmother in order to fit the child into the system that had been set up to help. Knowing the background was important from both the teacher's point of view and the counselor's.

Penny was not a discipline problem, but she could have become one

Take action when the problem is still small. Too often, a school counselor is not called in until there is a serious behavior problem. When we met with the "Mrs. Fredette" of this story, she talked about this. "Penny was not a discipline problem," she told us, "but she easily could have become one as she became more and more frustrated. Many kids, by the time they get to us, have become unmanageable. They have, in many cases, been rejected by their parents, and too often they know their grandparents don't really want them. It's no wonder they strike out at everyone around them. They don't need punishment, they need help, and most of all, they need to know someone cares."

4

Lenny

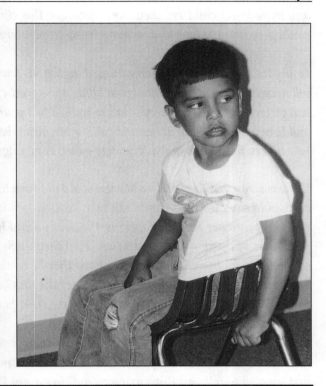

"You're mean! I hate you! I want to go live somewhere else!"

"You're mean! I hate you! I want to go live somewhere else!" Marcia's heart sank. Another tantrum! Six year old Lenny's face was contorted with anger, his body was stiff, his voice shrill.

This outburst seemed to be the worst yet. When she and Gil had agreed to accept Lenny as a foster child, they had known it wouldn't be easy, but not how hard it would be.

Lenny had been in nine foster homes. *In his short life, Lenny had been in nine foster homes. The courts had taken him away from his own mother when* *he was two years old. Lenny's social worker, Doreen, was a friend of Marcia's, and had told her about this bright, unhappy child, who was becoming more and more of a problem. Although Marcia and Gil had decided not to take on any more foster children, they were moved by this child's story. Perhaps they could give him the love and security he so desperately needed.*

Lenny had come to them, poorly dressed, toting his few meager possessions in a pillowcase. Now he had a nice room of his own, good clothes and a bicycle they had given him for his birthday. Marcia and Gil had poured out their love on him, and here he was yelling at her and calling her mean, because she had refused to take him to the mall to buy a Nintendo game. How ungrateful could he be?

Gil was away that weekend, so Marcia could not turn to him for support. Afraid she would say things she could not take back, she walked away from the angry child and into her bedroom, locking the door behind her. Tears ran down her face, tears of despair and frustration. Had they made a mistake? Was Lenny so damaged by his unhappy background that he could no longer be reached? Or was she just not strong enough to meet the task? She barely heard Lenny banging on the door and calling to her as she cried herself free of the pain.

As her sobs subsided, she wiped away the tears and picked up the phone. "Mom?" she asked as the phone was answered. "I'm so glad you're home. I just wanted to tell you I'm sorry for anything mean I ever said to you when I was a child. I didn't know how much it hurt."

He has no way of realizing how much he is hurting me. *After she hung up, her own words echoed in her ear. It's the same with Lenny, she thought. He has no way of realizing how much he is hurting me. Just then she heard strange scratching noises outside the room. She unlocked her door and opened it. There was Lenny, an oversized screwdriver in his hand, trying to remove the door hinge.*

"Are you all right?" he asked anxiously. "I was afraid something had happened to you."

Marcia got down on her knees and hugged him. "I'm all right, sweetheart, and so are you," she assured him. "I'm hungry. Let's go have some milk and cookies."

Understanding the problem

When Marcia went back to talk to Doreen, her friend told her what she had already begun to figure out. "Lenny has been shunted from one place to another. He has lost faith in grown-ups. He no longer believes he is ever going to have a mother and father who will love him no matter what he does. If things seem to be going well, he figures he might as well be as bad as he can and get it over with. He is afraid to care too much because he expects to be sent away again."

Lenny needed time to learn to trust. Marcia and Gil had to be prepared for many difficult days. Understanding why Lenny behaved as he did would help them to be patient, but that was not enough. They had to plan ahead, not just what they would do when the tantrums came, but plan for ways to avert trouble. How could they teach Lenny that there were better ways to deal with his own hurt and anger?

Planning to avoid future trouble

Reasonable rules. The first step was to lay down some reasonable rules, and as much as possible, include Lenny in making those rules. They could hardly say "No tantrums!" since that was not something Lenny could control at that point. Instead, Rule Number One might be, "When we say NO, listen to our reasons."

Let's look at the incident that upset Marcia. Lenny wanted to go to the Mall and buy a Nintendo game. Marcia said NO. What would her reasons be, and how could she help a six year old understand them?

Reason #1—A Nintendo game is expensive. Just the basic equipment in which to put the game cartridges would be anywhere from eighty to one hundred and sixty dollars, and the cartridges to be put in for individual games would be thirty to sixty dollars each. Marcia could explain this by using some comparisons that Lenny could understand. "We spend about eighty dollars a week for food. A Super-Nintendo would be two weeks of food. Do you think we could stop eating for two weeks?

"It costs us about one hundred and fifty dollars a week to rent this house. If we don't pay that, we can't live here.

"Out of the money Gil earns we pay for rent, food, clothes, gas for the car, oil for the furnace so we can stay warm, lights and our telephone. If we are careful, we have a little left over for extras. We put some of that aside each week and save it for something special. That's how we got your bicycle. It would take us at least two months to save enough for a Nintendo. Then we could only get you one game a month to play, and that wouldn't leave any money for Gil and me to buy things we want. Do you think that's fair?"

Reason #2—Marcia and Gil don't want Lenny to have a Nintendo game. Marcia and Gil might feel that Nintendo was not a good thing for Lenny to have. That would be valid from her point of view, but a lot harder to explain. Instead, she and Gil could try to provide options—other ways of having fun. Children love to have adults spend time with them. Board games like Parchesi and Aggravation; reading aloud, maybe a chapter a night from an exciting book; a game of catch in the backyard; sledding in the winter or swimming in the summer are all wonderful ways to spend time with a child. A child can be weaned away from passive activities when you give him other choices and share yourself with him.

Reason #3—Sometimes you just have to say NO. Marcia and Gil would explain that there are many good reasons, and give him some examples.

- ◆ "No, you cannot ride your bicycle on the main street. Traffic is too heavy, and it is dangerous."

- ◆ "No, you cannot stay up till ten o'clock every night. Your body needs sleep to stay healthy."

- ◆ "No, you cannot go out to play in the snow. You were sick yesterday, and the doctor said you had to stay in for a whole day after your fever went down."

- ◆ "No, I cannot take you to the park. I have a bad headache and I need to rest."

Firmness and consistency are necessary. Once the rules have been set, firmness and consistency are essential. No anger, no shouting, just "I'm sorry, Lenny, but that is against the rules."

A child with a temper often hits or kicks. They had to let Lenny know they wouldn't let him hurt himself or others *because* they loved him. A child needs and wants the adults in his life to set limits. It is a frightening thing to feel that no one cares enough to stop you from doing what is wrong.

The magic formula is love

Here are some ways to show it.

♦ A hug, a warm smile, a wink.

♦ Time shared, whether it is digging up a garden, helping clean up the house for company or just taking a quiet walk together.

♦ A positive approach. "Grandma's coming over. Let's see if we can make the living room look nice before she gets here," instead of "Go pick up the mess in the living room."

♦ Sharing decisions and family plans: where to go for a family outing, what color to paint his room, which shirt to buy.

All children need this "touch of love," not just those who have been abused, neglected or rejected.

Labels can do a lot of harm

At school, Lenny's behavior led to a battery of tests and interviews, from which it was decided that he was "emotionally disabled" (in the past, the term was "emotionally disturbed"). But labels can do a lot of harm. Put Yolanda with a "slow" class, and she soon comes to believe she is "dumb," and stops trying. Let Lenny know he is "emotionally disabled," and he may think of himself as a "bad kid" and do his best to live up to that label.

If we have to have labels at all, let's use "bright," "talented," "creative," "hardworking." Let children work to fulfill those images of themselves!

Both school and home following the same guidelines

Marcia and Gil shared with Lenny's teacher what they were doing and urged her to follow the same guidelines. His misbehavior at school was the result of his general unhappiness. Once he felt sure of his place in a family, once he knew he was loved and wasn't going to be sent away, his behavior at school improved noticeably. Of course, he did not become a model child at once. A child who has been hurting for six years isn't going to be cured overnight, but caring adults can affect that cure.

The happy ending to this true story is that Marcia and Gil decided to give up foster parenting and become adoptive parents. They adopted Lenny, and now he knows that he really belongs, that he is part of a family, and that he always will be.

"She has only one good day a week!"

"Here, let me help you with this," said Alice Milner, approaching four year old Shelley with a painting cover-up in her hand. To herself she was thinking, the child does look adorable in that red velveteen dress, with her black hair and eyes, but it's hardly suitable for school.

"No!" screamed Shelley, pulling away from her. "I won't wear that dumb old shirt. My daddy gave me this dress. He said I could wear it."

"But you might get paint on your pretty dress," said the teacher in reasonable tones.

"No, I won't! I know how to paint. Go away!" Shelley's screams had become piercing shrieks. The other children stopped their play, looking alarmed. Rather than have any more disruption, Alice stepped back and said no more.

Five minutes later, Shelley's voice again dominated the room. "You bumped me. You made me get paint on my dress!" Before the teacher could get to her, she reached out and made a black streak across Vicki's pink jersey.

Alice took the brush out of her hand before she could do any more damage. "I didn't bump her," sobbed Vicki, looking in dismay at the streak of paint.

At this point Shelley burst into tears and sobs that were close to hysteria. "My daddy will be mad at me," she cried, trembling all over.

Alice put her arm around Shelley's shoulders and drew her away from the others. "It's all right, Vicki," she said over her shoulder. "I will wash out the paint. Don't cry."

"What is happening?" asked a quiet voice, and Alice was relieved to see Mrs. Hanrahan, her director, standing in the doorway. The older woman's experienced eye was quick to assess the situation. "Shelley, you come with me," she said firmly. "Alice, you take care of Vicki. I'll send someone in to cover during nap time, and we'll talk then."

When Alice went into the office later, she sank into a chair with a sigh of relief. "I sure could tell this was a Monday!" she exclaimed. "What kind of magic did you use? Shelley was pretty calm when she came back. She ate her lunch and settled down for a nap with hardly any protest."

Irma Hanrahan's eyes twinkled. "My most useful magic," she said. "My lap and a rocking chair. Works wonders with children who are upset. Tell me, what did you mean about Monday?"

"Every Monday Shelley is wild." *Alice shrugged. "I'm not sure what's going on," she said, "but every Monday, Shelley is wild. She seems to look for trouble, and won't respond to anything I try."*

"Just Monday?" asked the other. "How about the rest of the week?"

"Tuesday is a little better, and Wednesday she seems to fit right in and enjoy herself, but Thursday she keeps asking for her mommy or daddy, and Friday is almost as bad as Monday. Come to think of it, Shelley only has one good day a week."

Sharing helpful information

The director looked troubled. "I should have talked to you about this before, but I didn't realize quite how bad the situation was," she said. "It's hard to find the right balance between protecting the parents' privacy and keeping the teacher informed.

"Shelley is an only child. Her parents were divorced a year ago, and six months ago her mother remarried. Shelley lives with her mother and stepfather, and spends weekends with her birth father. Her mother is trying hard to make her new marriage work, and has been successful to the point where, she assures me, the child is beginning to love her new father. But she also loves her own father, and her mother. Her dad, at the same time, has his daughter only two days a week. He is trying to build a strong bond with her so that she won't begin to forget him, so he does things like buy her fancy dresses. Poor Shelley has a lot of conflicting feelings to deal with; and probably a lot of questions she can't answer. Was it her fault her daddy went away? Is she supposed to do what he says, even if she knows her mother would say no? Is it all right to love her new daddy?"

Now what do I do?

"Thank you for telling me," exclaimed Alice, "and I promise I won't gossip about it. Now I understand why she acts the way she does, but I'm not sure what to do about it. Should I just give in to her no matter what she does? That doesn't seem right, and it doesn't seem fair to the other children."

Anticipate when she will need extra attention. *"No, you don't ignore it when Shelley breaks the rules," said the other woman. "You can anticipate that she will be in a bad state on Monday, so you need to be prepared. Think about your program. Try to involve her right away in things she likes to do, but things that are soothing, not stimulating. Does she like to play with the dress-up clothes, or rock the dolls? Hold her on your lap while you read a story to several children. If you want her to do something, do it first. You could say, 'I guess I'll put on an apron so I won't get anything on my clothes. I would hate to spoil the pretty shirt I have on.' She is much more apt to follow your lead than to do what you tell her to do.*

Help her release anger and frustration. *"Think of some ways to help her release anger and frustration. Dictating a story to you about how she feels is one good way. Most children like that because it gives them a feeling of control. Another wonderful way to calm a child is water play. Put some warm water in the sink with a little soap, and let her wash the tea set from the housekeeping corner.*

Consistency is important. *"Above all, give her consistency— something that is missing in her life. She should be part of the decision-making about the rules of the classroom, along with the others. Once the rules are set, she must learn to follow them, just as the others must. However, keep them simple and at a minimum, and never make an issue of something that really isn't important. Before you say 'No' or 'You can't' ask yourself if it really matters.*

Definition of discipline

"Remember the definition of discipline I gave you? The one I got from Grace Mitchell's book on discipline? **'Discipline is the slow, bit-by-bit, time consuming task of helping children see the sense in acting a certain way.'** *Keep the words 'slow' and 'bit-by-bit' in your mind. This problem isn't going to be solved overnight, but once Shelley learns that school is a good place to be, that you care about her, that things won't keep changing, you will find that the 'bad' part of the week will shrink, and the 'good' part will expand."*

6

Adam

> "I almost wish he would act up. He is becoming more and more withdrawn."

Beverly Dwyer, third grade teacher, tapped on the door marked School Adjustment Counselor. In answer to a muffled "Come in," she pushed the door open. "Can you spare a few minutes, Norm?" she asked.

"Sure. Have a seat," he offered. "What brings you to my office?"

"It's Adam Ames."

"Adam?" Norman Macrae looked at her in surprise. "I never hear a word about Adam. Is he giving you a problem?"

She shook her head. "It isn't that. I almost wish he would act up once in a while. He is just becoming more and more withdrawn. He does his work, but he never speaks up in class, he doesn't talk to the other children, he stays by himself at recess, and he just seems to have an air of—I don't know what to call it—unhappiness? remoteness? despair?"

"Have you talked with him? Does he know you are here?"

"I've tried to talk to him, but he pulls back—almost like a turtle going into its shell. No, I didn't tell him I was coming to see you. I didn't want him to think he was in trouble."

"Have you any idea what's behind this?" asked Norman.

"I think so," she said uneasily, "but I don't want to jump to conclusions. Adam's parents were divorced last year. During the summer his mother remarried, and he spends weekends and vacations there. His father kept the house and he remarried. During schooltime Adam lives with him and his new wife. His stepfather has three boys. His stepmother doesn't have any children of her own. I think the poor kid is floundering, trying to figure out what has happened and where he stands. Maybe he would talk to you."

"I'll have a word with the principal and see how she wants me to handle this," said Norman. "With her approval, I'll get in touch with the parents."

"Wouldn't you want to see Adam before the parents come in?" asked Beverly.

"I can't do a thing without the parents' permission," he explained. "I will probably say something like, 'It has come to my attention that Adam is becoming withdrawn. Would it be okay with you if I observe him in the classroom and either talk with him or get back to you?' The classic response to that is, 'Is he in trouble?' and I would assure them that he is not."

With permission from the parents, the school counselor observed Adam

The next morning, before school, he let Beverly know that the parents had given him permission to observe, and later that day he walked into the room. He moved around quietly, stopping to chat briefly with several different children, including Adam, but not calling attention to him. Another day he went onto the playground during recess, noticed Adam standing by himself off to one side, and was able to speak quietly with him, asking him to come see him that afternoon.

"I don't like being part of two families." *It took several visits to Norm's office before Adam would talk to him openly. He moved in steps, from refusing to speak at all about his home life, to "yes" and "no" answers, to brief statements. Norman sensed that Adam had a growing need to talk to someone about his feelings, and finally the dam broke. Once started, the words came tumbling out. "Why did this have to happen? I don't like being part of two families. I don't like it when I stay with my mother and them. My stepbrothers are bigger than I am, and they push me around. My mother never sticks up for me. She says, 'This is their home, we have to do things their way.' I love my mother, but I don't like living there, even part-time. And my mother doesn't like my stepmother. She's always asking about my stepmother, stuff like 'Does she make better spaghetti than I do? Does she buy you things? Is she prettier than I am? Does she let you stay up late?' And she says, 'She's not your mother. Remember, I'm your real mother.'"*

Adam stopped to catch his breath. His voice was trembling, and he was very close to tears.

Norman said in matter-of-fact tones, "It must be hard for you. But what about your stepmother? Do you like her? Is she good to you? Are you happy when you stay with your father?"

"Is it all right to love my stepmother?" *The boy nodded vigorously. "Yes, I am. They listen to me, you know? She helps me with my homework. She and my dad never fight. She's really swell. I wish I could stay there weekends, so we could do stuff together. But, she's not my mother, and I keep wondering, can you love two people at once, I mean, like two mothers? Is it all right to love my stepmother?"*

Working with the parents

They had not realized how withdrawn he was at school. Norman Macrae arranged an appointment with Adam's father and stepmother. Because Adam felt comfortable with them at home, and acted quite normally, they had not realized how withdrawn he was at school. With the cooperation of Mr. Ames, he was able to set up a meeting with him and his former wife. Although she was defensive and angry, she did agree to try to put less pressure on Adam, and to let Adam stay with his father one weekend a month.

Eventually, Beverly Dwyer was able to report that Adam was becoming part of the class, joining in with the other children's activities, and even—she laughed ruefully when she told him—getting into a little mischief now and then.

Things worked out because the parents cooperated. The school adjustment counselor who talked to me about Adam made it clear that things worked out well in that case because the parents cooperated. But what happens if the answer is, "No, you may not talk to my child"? The first thing, he said, is to ask the teacher to watch for any possible backlash, anything that might indicate that a child was being punished because of his call.

Whether this happened or not, if the condition that had first caused the teacher to be concerned continued or seemed to get worse, the next step could be for the principal to send a letter asking for a joint conference.

Supporting the child

A good school counselor supports both the teacher and the parents, coordinates any therapy needed, and above all, supports the child. Behavior such as Adam had been displaying often leads to a crisis, and the counselor can move quickly to help deal with that crisis. He can then follow through with a plan for meeting the needs of all concerned.

He did warn that sometimes, with all the adults cooperating, and with the best efforts of a skilled counselor, things still might not turn out as well as they did for Adam.

We must not expect miracles, but when a child's needs are becoming overwhelming, it is often an alert teacher who opens the door to finding help.

7

Laura

"Laura has been cheating."

"All right, Ms. Kingsley, I'll be there tomorrow at three," said Charlene Amato. "Thank you for calling me." *Now what is that all about, she wondered. Laura's never had any trouble in school, but her teacher says there is a problem.*

Clattering footsteps on the stairs brought her into the front hall. "Flavio! Leo! Where are you going?" she called as her two teenage stepsons headed for the front door.

"Out!" called the older boy over his shoulder. "We'll be back later."

"Have you done your homework?" she called, but the boys were already out of earshot.

Angry voices from the second floor sent her hurrying upstairs. As she neared the room her daughter shared with her stepsister, she heard twelve year old Gina's voice. "Leave my things alone. Keep your clothes on your side of the closet. Don't touch things on my bureau! And don't ever wipe your dirty hands on my towel!"

Laura's voice was just as loud. "You use most of the closet. There isn't room for my clothes. And I forgot which towel was yours. You're a selfish pig."

Charlene walked into the room without stopping to knock. Both girls were glaring at each other, their faces flushed with anger. Gina's black eyes were snapping, and her hand was raised as if to hit Laura. She let it fall when she saw Charlene, and turned away abruptly.

"Mama," cried eight year old Laura. "She was going to hit me. I didn't do anything wrong. I was just smelling her perfume, I didn't use any."

"Laura, you must not touch Gina's things," said Charlene firmly. "Remember, this was her room, and it's hard for her to have someone else sharing it." Just then a wail sounded from the next room. "Now see what you've done," she cried. "The baby is awake, and he was settled for the night."

She hurried in and took the crying baby out of his crib. "Shh, Jimmy, it's all right. Mummy's here," she murmured softly. As she walked around the room, holding the baby and patting his back soothingly, she thought despairingly, I can't handle this, a two month old baby, three stepchildren who wish they'd never seen me, and now my daughter is in trouble at school. It wouldn't be so bad if Tony were here, but with this new job, he's away all the time, it seems. This isn't working out.

Meeting with the teacher

The next afternoon she had to take the baby with her to the school. Ms. Kingsley had kept Laura, who was sitting at her desk, looking sullen. Seeing her through the teacher's eyes, Charlene was shocked. What is this, she wondered. Laura was always cheerful, always smiling. She looks really ugly with that frown on her face.

"What a beautiful baby!" exclaimed the teacher. "Laura didn't tell me she had a little brother."

Again Charlene felt a tremor of shock. She had assumed that Laura bragged about Jimmy at school. "Please tell me why you asked me to come in," she said, trying to sound calm.

Ms. Kingsley sighed. "I'm having a problem with Laura, and I hoped between us we could get to the bottom of it. Report cards come out in two weeks, and I'm afraid Laura's marks aren't going to be satisfactory."

"How can that be?" asked Charlene. "She's been getting A's and B's on her papers."

"Laura has been cheating." *"Yes," admitted the teacher. "Unfortunately, I have realized that Laura has been cheating. She has been copying from other children or keeping notes tucked in her hand. I'm not sure just how she has done it. When I started asking the class questions, and Laura couldn't give me answers about material she had just gotten an "A" paper on, I got suspicious. What I don't understand is why. Laura is smart enough to get "B's" and "C's" without cheating. I'm sure she wasn't doing this at the beginning of the year. Now I am wondering if it has anything to do with this new baby."*

"How could Laura shame her like this?" *Charlene was stunned. Her first reaction was anger. How could Laura shame her like this? But a look at her daughter, tears running down her face, a picture of misery, stopped her short.*

She thrust the baby toward the teacher. "Please hold him," she said, and opened her arms to Laura, who jumped up and hurled herself at her mother. For a few minutes Charlene just held her daughter in her arms until her sobs gave way to an occasional hiccup.

"Honey, I'm not mad at you," she said softly. "I'm upset because something is bothering you and I didn't know it, but I think it is my fault. Tell me what this is all about. I can guess part of it, but it will be better if you tell me."

Laura kept her face pressed against her mother, but both Charlene and Ms. Kingsley could hear her faltering voice.

"I thought you didn't love me any more." *"Everything's different," she muttered. "You never scold them. Whatever they do is okay, but whatever I do is wrong. You always take their side. I had my own room, too, until the baby came, and then I had to move in with Gina. It wasn't my idea. I'd rather sleep on the couch in the living room! You've forgotten all about Daddy, you love Tony now, you love the baby, and I thought you didn't love me any more."*

Charlene's own tears were streaming now. "Oh, darling, I love you more than you can imagine," she said. "I'll never forget your father, but it's been three years since he died, and I was very lonely when I met Tony. Loving him doesn't change what I felt for your dad. I've been trying too hard to be fair with Tony's children, and in doing that, I have cheated you. Which reminds me, how does this explain why you cheated?"

Ms. Kingsley spoke for the first time since she had taken the baby. "I think I can explain that," she said. "You thought if you took home some "A" papers, your mother would be pleased with you and pay more attention to you. Am I right?" Laura nodded.

What happens next?

"What's going to happen on the report card?" asked Charlene. "I know you can't give her marks based on the papers she cheated on, but do you have to fail her? I hate to have that on her record, even in third grade."

"No," agreed the teacher. "I wouldn't want to see that either, and I know Laura has been learning, in spite of herself and her unhappiness. I will mark her "C" on everything this time, and by the final card in June, she will have time to get back to her usual good work."

Blending two families

In spite of the hard time she had been having, Laura was a lucky girl. She had an understanding and flexible teacher. She also had a loving mother, who listened when it was necessary.

Charlene was indeed swamped by her responsibilities and by unexpectedly having to handle all the problems by herself most of the time. There were no easy answers for her.

She had been married to Tony for a year and a half. He had been a widower for a year when they met, and they were first drawn together by their mutual needs, but this soon turned to love on both sides. They knew there would be problems blending their two families, but hoped that a new baby would help draw the children together. Things had been going pretty well as long as Tony was around to handle his share of the inevitable problems, but he had lost his old job when the company he worked for was acquired, and he could not afford to give up the job he had found, even though he would have preferred to stay home more and not to have to travel. They had planned to buy a larger house after the baby was born, but with his lower salary there just was not enough money for that.

Charlene's mistake was natural and common. A mother assumes her child will *know* that she is loved, and is apt to put her efforts into establishing a bond with her husband's children. Charlene had forgotten to look at the situation through Laura's eyes. It is important, in combining two families, for each parent to spend some time with his or her own children, listening to their concerns and reassuring them.

Work out compromises at family meetings. There were some things they could do. When Tony was home, they could have family meetings, in which all the children could talk about their feelings, and they could try together to work out compromises.

A new baby can be a bridge between two family groups or can widen the gulf. All the children should be included in talk about the new baby, planning for it, giving more help as the pregnancy draws to an end, and in caring for the baby after it is born. Only then does it become "our" baby. If, in a family meeting, Charlene and Tony had posed the problem of where the baby's crib, changing table and clothes would be, Gina and Laura might have offered to share a room. As it was, they both felt they had lost their space, and resented it.

Keep a few cherished traditions from each family and develop new ones. To avoid the "But we always did it this way," that can cause friction, especially around the holidays, they could agree to keep one or two of the most cherished traditions from each family, and to start some new ones of their own.

Family counseling would help all of them, including grief counseling. It is generally agreed that it takes from one to seven years to deal with the death of a parent or spouse.

Along with their other problems, they were trying to blend two families, a process that can take two to four years, or more. Charlene and Tony, as the adults, need to draw on all their parenting skills, and to recognize that it takes love, patience, understanding and *time* to create a new family.

8

Joshua & Howie

"What shocked Helen was the knife in Joshua's hand."

Helen Freeman was watching carefully to make sure no child ran in front of the swings and got knocked down, when screams of panic sent her racing across the playground. A moment before, her class had been playing an exuberant game of tag. Now they were clustered in a circle around something she could not see. "Not another fight," she thought despairingly. "That's the third time this week."

She pushed through the children, ready to pull a couple of struggling, punching children apart—and stopped short in horror. Howie was on his feet, circling warily, one arm up defensively, his face a mixture of anger and fear. Half *crouching before him, as if ready to leap, was Joshua. From his lips came a shocking stream of obscenities, but the thing that had frozen Helen in place was the sharp knife in Joshua's hand and the blood dripping from Howie's other arm.*

Finding her voice, she sprang into the circle between the two boys, faced Joshua and said in her most authoritative voice, "Joshua! Put that knife down— NOW!"

The child's eyes blazed as he glared at her, but she stood firm, and after a heart-stopping moment he opened his clenched fist and the knife dropped to the ground.

Gratefully, Helen heard running feet and the voice of Ruth Silva, the gym teacher.

"My God," gasped the other, as she took in the situation, "what's going on here? Are you hurt?"

"No, but Howie is." Now that the crisis was over, Helen's knees felt weak, but she kept her voice steady as she said to the other children, "All of you go over to Ms. Rollins and stay with her until someone comes out."

The children ran off, and Helen turned to Ruth. "Will you take Joshua, along with the knife, into the office while I get Howie to the nurse?"

Howie's was shaking and crying as Helen put her arm around him and led him into the building. Once the school nurse had taken a good look at the deep cut in Howie's arm and put on a tourniquet to stop the bleeding, she rushed him off to the hospital. Helen went to the office.

Henry Riggs, the principal, met her at the door. "Are you sure you're not hurt?" he asked.

"I'm not hurt, but I'll admit I do feel shaky," she responded.

Howie was taunting him, calling him stupid. *He led her to a chair. "I don't know whether to scold you or to commend you. You could have been seriously hurt, but I guess I would have done the same thing myself. Now, first of all, my secretary has gone out to take your class inside, and she will stay with them until you can go back. I have also called both boys' parents. Howie's mother has gone to the hospital. Joshua's mother and father are coming here. Joshua tells me this started because Howie has been making fun of him every day— taunting him because he can't read, calling him stupid. Today, Joshua decided to put a stop to it."*

Helen Freeman's concern showed on her face. "Mr. Riggs, there's been a lot more fighting than usual this year, but this! I still can't believe it, and I can't believe I'm still teaching second grade!"

Calling an emergency meeting for all teachers

Henry Riggs called an emergency meeting of all teachers that afternoon. "I know you have all heard about the trouble we had this morning," he began. "First of all, Howie was treated at the hospital and released. He will probably have a scar on his arm, but there was no permanent damage. Bad as this was, we can all be grateful that it wasn't more serious.

"As for Joshua, the police department's Juvenile Detective, Mr. Holt, came right over, and was here when Joshua's parents arrived. I have suspended Joshua for three days so Mr. Holt, Joshua's parents, the school psychologist and I can meet to decide what comes next. We will have to meet with Howie's mother, too. Both boys are going to need counseling.

What are we going to do about violence in our school?

Violence in our school is on the increase. *"A number of you have come to me this year to report problems in your rooms—fighting, bullying, open insolence to you—and I have worked with you in each case. Now I think it's time for all of us to look at the whole picture. We all know violence among children in a school setting is a growing problem across the country, but I guess we thought it couldn't happen here. Well, now it has, and I want to know what is going on right here in our school, and what we are going to do about it!"*

Gather information about the television viewing habits of the children. *For a few minutes everyone was silent. Then Sam Turowski, a fourth grade teacher, spoke up. "I think it's television," he said. "Sometimes when the kids are coming in to the room in the morning, I hear them talking about television shows they watched the night before. They seem fascinated by cop shows with high speed chases and lots of shooting."*

Another teacher chimed in. "It isn't just the cop shows. I hear them using language I wouldn't have thought they would even know."

"What if we all take a survey? Let's try to find out what shows they are watching, in all the grades. Then we should watch some of those programs ourselves and see what messages the kids are getting," suggested someone else.

"Good idea," approved the principal. "Today is Thursday. Next Thursday we'll meet again and compare information."

Most children watched television without supervision or limits. *It was a sober and shaken group that faced Henry Riggs the next week. Their reports were very similar. Most of the children, even the very young ones, were allowed to watch television without supervision or limits. Many of them stayed up until nine or ten and watched whatever their parents were watching.*

To get this information, the teachers had all started discussions in their classroom about favorite shows, or what the children had seen the night before. "The thing that frightens me," said one woman, "is that pain and death don't have any real meaning for them. It's just a show. A man can be beaten brutally, but five minutes later he's back at the chase. A woman can be killed in a movie, but two days later they see her in another movie, or another program. It's like it's all a game."

"They are being taught that violence is the way to solve problems."
"That's not all," added another voice. "They are being taught that violence is the way to solve problems. If you aren't strong enough to beat up someone, you use a gun or a knife."

Ruth Silva said thoughtfully, "We tell our children the police are the 'good guys.' Then they see the police beating people, shooting people. I think that says to them that it's all right to hurt someone if you think you are right and the other person is wrong. Doesn't every child believe he's right when he's fighting with another kid?"

"Why didn't Joshua go to Helen or Mr. Riggs for help?" asked Flo Haskell, one of the younger teachers in the school.

"That's a boy thing," said Al Prentice. "Boys think they have to be tough. Even young ones know you just don't 'rat' on another boy. You fight your own fights. I don't think we can blame that all on television. It's been going on for a long, long time. However, I do think the television shows reinforce the idea."

"It isn't just the boys who think it's wrong to 'rat on someone,' as you put it," protested Ruth Silva. "Another thing—what about fear? Joshua may have been afraid that if he got Howie in trouble, he might be beaten up by Howie's pals. You see a lot of that on shows about 'bad guys.'"

Working with parents

Get parents involved. *Mr. Riggs took over again. "Television certainly isn't the only thing we have to look at, but it's probably the most universal. I'd like you all to put on paper everything you've learned: the names of the shows, the examples of violence, what percent of the children in your room watched those programs. Then we'll compile it all and present it to the parents in a meeting. We didn't realize how widespread and serious this problem is, and I'm sure the parents don't realize it either. We'll lay out the facts and appeal to them to work with us by monitoring the television their children watch. No matter what we decide to do, it won't work unless the parents get involved."*

Share ideas. Henry Riggs took the first important step when he spoke to his staff as co-workers, rather than announcing his decisions. "We are in this together," he was saying, "but you are on the front lines. Give me your thoughts; I will listen. Let's share our ideas."

A first step for the teachers could be to look at what lay behind Joshua's attack on Howie. A lawyer could have argued that there was provocation. Howie taunted him. Joshua felt humiliated, and he didn't know how to react except with violence. After all, he had seen plenty of "models" for that on television. Had he ever seen, on television or in real life, an example of two people settling their differences peacefully?

What can a teacher do to prevent violence?

Pay attention to teasing. Miss Freeman was undoubtedly aware that Joshua was lagging behind most of the class in developing reading skills, but was she sensitive to the way he felt about it? Was she paying attention to the way Howie, and maybe others, were teasing Joshua?

Build children's self-confidence. If she had recognized these things, what could she have done about it? Without being obvious, she could have looked for Joshua's strengths, used them to build his self-confidence, and thus help him gain the respect of his peers. Being a slow starter in reading does not have to mean a child is "dumb." Did Joshua like baseball? He may have known all about the players and their records. She could have used that knowledge, asking questions he could answer quickly, making the others aware of his expertise in that area.

She was probably already giving Joshua extra help in reading, but was she talking to him about it, explaining how certain things could help, and letting him know she was going to go right on looking for ways to close the gap between his reading ability and that of his classmates?

What can all early childhood teachers do to prevent violent confrontations?

Help children accept their differences. "Today let's look at the boys in this room. How many of you are six years old? Stand up. You are all six; are you all the same size? No, Anton is about four inches taller than Clyde. But growing is a funny thing. Four years from now, Clyde may be as tall as Anton.

"Who are the fastest runners? Who can throw a ball the farthest? Who are the best spellers? Can any of you play the guitar?

"Did you know that Manolo speaks two languages, Italian and English? Can anyone else speak two languages?

"You are all good at something, but different things, and that's the way it's supposed to be."

Talk about feelings. Preschool teachers start talking about this with their three year olds, and children who have had that in their background are less apt to have the kind of trouble Joshua and Howie had in second grade. A teacher tries to give three year olds words to express their feelings, and to make them aware that using the wrong words can hurt people. At seven, a lot of children need the same things but are capable of more understanding. You talk about what makes them feel good and what makes them feel bad. About having friends. About how good it makes them feel when they do something that makes someone else happy. About the words they can use to let others know how they feel.

Teach children to work together. It is important to help children develop a sense of community, and one way to do that is to have them work with a partner or in small groups. They help each other, and divide up the work. The teacher must make sure that each member of the group working on a project has a role to play, a responsibility.

Provide a safe environment. Children hear their parents talking; they see things on the evening news that are frightening. They need to know that the people in charge will make sure no guns or knives are going to be used against them, and if this does happen, they need to see that prompt action is taken.

They have been warned about strangers and have heard about people coming into a school and abducting children. They may worry—can this happen to me? In one school we visited, every person who enters the school and is not on the regular staff *must* wear a badge. Some badges say Volunteer, some say Tutor, some say Visitor, but every child in that school knows that an adult without a badge is someone who doesn't belong there, and should be reported at once.

There's another kind of safety they need—to know they won't be hurt in non-physical ways. The following create an atmosphere that leads to a more subtle form of violence:

♦ Books, television programs and video games that promote gender discrimination.

♦ Insulting remarks about other children, especially those with a disability of some kind.

These things cause pain and resentment that bring a child to the point where he may become so fearful that he can't function in either academic or social ways, or he may finally strike back in the way Joshua did.

In the battle against violence, both teachers and parents need to be on the watch for actions which hurt others, teach that such behavior is wrong and teach the victims how to respond.

A plan for the whole school

Evening meetings for parents. The school planned a series of evening meetings with parents to show how positive approaches could eliminate the need for children to feel angry and aggressive. To support the actions of the teachers, the following areas were emphasized with the parents.

Respect differences. Go over the techniques suggested for teachers, but also bring up the importance of recognizing and respecting the customs of different cultures; understanding that skin color is not a measure of worth; accepting the appearance and actions of children with disabilities. Stress the fact that people have more similarities than differences, and the similarities are what count.

Model how to express feelings. Show how adults, through their own behavior, can teach children how to handle their feelings.

- ♦ By letting children see them apologize for a hasty, insensitive remark.

- ♦ By telling children how they feel when kids are rude or disobedient.

- ♦ By letting children see them settle differences with other adults reasonably and calmly.

- ♦ By respecting children's feelings, and expecting to be respected themselves.

Value children working together. It may be hard for parents who grew up in schools where children sat in their own seats, did their own work, and never talked, to accept the idea of letting children work in groups of four or five, talk about their ideas and share their information. Only if the teachers believe in it, can they convince parents of the benefits, but it can be done!

You, the parents and teachers, can make a difference if every day you show the children at home or in your class that you like them, appreciate them, respect them and are proud of them. You'll be surprised how hard they'll work to keep you feeling that way, and when you get children working on goals like these, you will see a dramatic improvement in overall behavior.

9

Felipe

"The teacher said I was rude."

Felipe Garza was worried. It was a Wednesday, and usually he hurried home on Wednesday because that was the day Mama made cookies. But today his feet were dragging. How could he tell Mama his teacher had been mad at him? How could he explain it, when he didn't understand it himself? And what if Daddy were home? He'd get spanked for sure, because Daddy said the teacher was always right and you must never argue or be naughty.

Last year in kindergarten, Felipe had loved school. Miss Sanchez was so nice, and she taught him many things. But this year he had a new teacher. She had come from someplace in the north, where it was cold and snowed in winter.

She had yellow hair and blue eyes. She was very pretty, but she sure got mad easily. He still didn't know what he had done. She said he was rude, but he hadn't meant to be.

Lucia Garza knew something was wrong the minute Felipe came in the door. She sat down and held out her arms, and he rushed into them, the pent-up sobs bursting out. She let him cry for a few minutes, holding him close. When he quieted down, she handed him a tissue from her apron pocket, and said briskly, "Now, what was that all about?"

He hung his head. "The teacher scolded me. She said I was rude."

"What?" exclaimed Lucia. "What did you do?"

"She said I wouldn't look at her. And I called her ma'am. She said not to call her ma'am. She said you had to go to the school and talk to her. But I wasn't trying to be rude. Is Daddy going to spank me?"

"No," said his mother firmly. "You were not naughty. I will go to the school all right, and I will talk to her. Don't you worry about it any more. Come have a cookie, then you can go out and play."

Lucia was rather mad herself that night when she told her husband, Roberto, what had happened. "These young teachers!" she fumed. "They come down here from Boston and New York and they think they know everything. Why don't they try to learn how it is here? If they want to teach Hispanic children, why don't they learn our ways?"

He shrugged. "You think our girls would do any better if they went up north to teach?" he asked mildly. "They are just young. They will learn. You go and explain to this teacher."

Talking with the teacher

Explain traditions and cultures. *The next morning Lucia walked to the school early with Felipe, so she could talk to Miss Johnson before the day began. She had calmed down and was able to speak in a pleasant voice.*

"In our culture," she explained, "children are taught to keep their eyes down when they speak to grown-ups. It is considered rude for them to look directly at an adult. To us, that seems bold. Also, they always use the words, 'Yes, ma'am' or 'Yes, sir' to show respect. Felipe could not understand why you were telling him to do something that he would have been scolded for at home."

The young teacher blushed. "I am sorry, Felipe," she said. "I didn't realize. I won't make that mistake again. I hope we can be friends."

He beamed at her. "Si," he agreed. "That is good."

Respecting customs and traditions of different groups

There are, of course, a number of groups that fall into the category of Hispanics, and each group has its own traditions and customs. The family in this story was Mexican-American, and they lived in the southwest.

Our information about this cultural group comes from Connie Rocha, who is herself Mexican-American. She and her husband have raised five children; she owns and directs a child care center which is open to all, but is especially popular with parents who want their children to know and be proud of their Mexican heritage—something the school emphasizes. She teaches courses in Early Childhood Education at a Community College and is in demand as a conference speaker. She is on the school board of a large city, and is widely known by educators.

What do you do when a teacher insists on behavior that contradicts what is taught at home?

According to Connie's observations and studies, about two-thirds of the Mexican-Americans in her community adhere to the ways they learned from their parents. Children are taught to honor their parents, and it is impressed upon them at an early age that teachers are very important people, to be trusted and respected. For this reason, it is especially difficult for the children when they have a teacher who insists on behavior that contradicts what they have been taught at home.

Connie told us about another case. Both parents were very upset because a note had come home from school asking them to come in to talk about their son's behavior. The teacher was an Anglo, and the parents felt uncertain of themselves and how to talk to her. They begged Connie to go and find out what their son had done.

Connie did go, and explained to the teacher who she was and why she was there. "What did Miguel do that was so bad that you had to send a note home?" she asked.

"Well, it wasn't really that bad," said the teacher. "He and another boy were whispering together while I was talking. It's just that Miguel is in my top group, and usually behaves very well. I thought it best to nip in the bud any tendency toward bad behavior."

"Well, you created a major upset at home," said Connie. "I feel sure you could have taken care of the matter by talking to Miguel. But tell me, what do you mean by 'top group'? How are the children grouped?"

Keep expectations high for all children

"The top group includes any Mexican-American children who speak and understand English very well. They may understand Spanish, but they don't use it in school. The middle group is for children who speak English fairly well, but still speak Spanish quite a bit of the time. I'm not always sure they understand me, and since my own Spanish is not very strong, I don't always understand them. The low group is the ones who speak very little English and, while in school, speak Spanish most of the time."

*Connie looked at her. "Tell me," she said carefully, trying to hide her dismay and anger, "if you were to take a course with a Mexican-American teacher who divided her class as you have, but put those fluent in Spanish in the top group, you would probably be in the bottom group. How would that make **you** feel?"*

The teacher reddened. "But what else can I do?" she protested. "I can't teach the children who don't speak English the same things I teach the others. I concentrate on helping them improve their English."

Connie threw up her hands in a gesture of exasperation. "So you not only put them in the low group, you make sure they stay there by limiting what you teach them!" she exclaimed. "Have you ever considered teaching them as a whole class—teaching the same things to all of them, and letting those who speak both English and Spanish help the others? And have you considered working to improve your own Spanish? And having meetings with parents aimed at learning more about their ways?"

Learn about different cultures

In today's mobile population, teachers move, and so do families. Children who have lived in Boston all their young lives may find themselves in Connie's community with a Mexican-American teacher, or vice versa.

This country is one of diversity, and *any* teacher, from preschool up, may work with children of many racial and ethnic backgrounds. It is up to the teacher to learn the ways of other cultures, and to treat *all* of the children in the class with respect and understanding.

10

Lynette

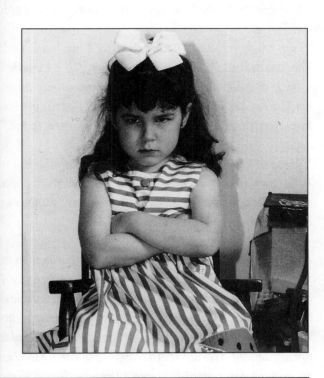

> *"I don't have to if I don't want to."*

"Goodbye, Lynette, I'll see you tomorrow," Gloria Caporino called after the last youngster to leave the child care center with her mother.

"It wouldn't break my heart if you never came back," she muttered under her breath. "Thank goodness Mrs. Lindstadt wasn't late tonight. Perhaps Ms. M. will have time to talk with me."

She hesitated in the open door of the director's office, and Ms. Mancuso looked up. Ms. M., as she was affectionately known to her teachers, had a warm smile and expressive brown eyes that could twinkle with amusement, soften with sympathy, or flash with indignation.

"You look quite tired, Gloria. Is it the heat? Would you like a glass of iced tea?"

"I am worn out, and I'd love some iced tea, but it isn't really the heat that has knocked me out," answered the teacher. "It's Lynette Lindstadt, that little girl who just walked by your door. She may look angelic, but she is the most contentious, disagreeable three year old I have ever had in my class. She's only been here three days, but she has really gotten to me."

"Those are harsh words to describe a child who has only been on this earth a little over thirty-six months," said the older woman mildly. "This doesn't sound like you. You're an excellent teacher. How is Lynette different from the other children you have had?"

Gloria sipped her iced tea, searching for words to explain herself. "I guess she took me by surprise," she said finally. "When she first came Monday, she looked like a doll, with her dark curls and pretty dress. She waved goodbye to her mother with no signs of concern, and I thought, no problems with this one. Was I ever wrong! From the word go, she has refused to cooperate and has been openly defiant. Her standard response to every direction has been, 'I don't want to, and if I don't want to, I don't have to.'"

"Can you be more specific?" asked Ms. Mancuso, pulling a note pad toward her, and jotting down notes as Gloria went on.

"She wouldn't come to the circle for our morning meeting, but went wandering around the room, taking toys off shelves and leaving them on the floor; she wouldn't put on a smock for painting; she wouldn't put away the blocks after playing with them; she wouldn't wash her hands after going to the bathroom or before eating; after lunch, she wouldn't take her dirty dishes to the counter with the other children; she didn't want to go out to the playground, but once out, she wouldn't come in when it was time; she wouldn't lie down on a cot for a nap. Oh, she did go out to the playground eventually, and come in again, *but I've been arguing with her about everything, and it's frustrating. Today I suggested that she wear play clothes, perhaps shorts, in this hot weather, and she said flatly, 'I like dresses. I don't want to wear shorts, and if I don't want to, I don't have to.'"*

Working out a strategy with the director

Save the NO's for the important things. *The director nodded sympathetically. "No wonder you are exhausted. You have been having a tough time. I know how effective you have been with other difficult children. You said Lynette took you by surprise. Perhaps that's what threw you off balance. Have you tried the path of least resistance? Save the absolute no's for the places where they are imperative and yield on those that don't affect anyone's health or safety. When she refuses to join the circle, offer alternatives. Say, 'We'd love to have you join us in the circle, but if not, here are some things you may do instead. You may play with the dolls, or look at a book or color. I'll give you some paper and crayons if you want to draw pictures.' At nap time, offer her a book to look at quietly. You know, you can always suggest that she take a doll to my office and rock in my rocking chair.*

Involve the other children. *"Of course, you can't bend on hand washing, but you could pick two children to show her how they make soap gloves. You probably talked to her about the health reasons for washing, but also try drawing in the other children by asking them why we wash. Sometimes hearing other children explain rules is more effective than doing it yourself. As for puting the blocks away, try joining her and making a game of it. 'This long one goes right here. Can you find another one like it?' If she absolutely refuses that approach, then it is time to say,' If you don't put away the things you play with, others can't enjoy them. Tomorrow you may not play with the blocks.'"*

Gloria sighed heavily. "You're right. Of course, I know all those things, I just lost my cool and forgot to apply them. I'm embarrassed to admit that I let a three year old child get me so upset."

"Don't be, we've all been there," Ms. M. replied with a laugh. "So tomorrow you will start again, but don't expect instant results. She may have only been here three days, but the behavior she brought with her was established long before you saw her. By the way, does she try to hurt other children, or spoil their work?"

"No, but she isn't winning any friends. She is bossy—everything has to be her way."

"Hmm, yes, that fits with her other behavior. Well, I think our next step is to ask the parents to come in for a conference. They both work, so it may mean our staying late or coming in early. Are you willing to do that?"

"Absolutely," said Gloria promptly. "I would gladly give up half an hour if it would make life easier from then on. Besides, I really do want to help Lynette. She is going to have a hard time if she doesn't learn to get along with others."

The parents both had busy days

By the end of the day Velma felt drained. *Velma Lindstadt was an appointment secretary in a busy medical clinic, working from nine to five. All day she had to remain patient and smiling as she tried to please people who needed, or thought they needed, to see a doctor immediately. One of the doctors was a pediatrician, and Velma's heart went out to some of the very young patients who sat in the waiting room, wide-eyed and frightened. By the end of a day, she often felt drained.*

Sven worked long hours. *The Child Care Center was only a few miles away, so she was usually able to pick up Lynette by 5:15. Her husband, Sven, had a more irregular schedule. He and a partner had started their own construction company. Sven was strong and healthy, and didn't seem to mind the hard work, but his hours were long, and he was ready to relax when he got home.*

On this particular day, Velma pretty much ignored Lynette's chatter as they drove home. Her mind was focused on the tasks that lay ahead of her. She had taken a chicken out of the freezer that morning. She would stuff that and get it in the oven. I might even have time for a glass of wine to help me unwind, she thought. Dinner won't be ready until about eight or later; Sven should be home by then. I'd better give Lynette a snack to hold her.

She pulled into the driveway with a sigh of relief, glad to be out of the traffic. "Come in and have a banana and a glass of milk," she said to her daughter. "Dinner won't be ready for quite a while."

Lynette shook her head. "I don't want a banana," she said petulantly, and instead helped herself to a bag of potato chips and a soda and settled down in front of the television. Velma sighed, but didn't feel up to arguing the point.

Sven came in around seven. After a quick shower he came into the kitchen and took a soda from the refrigerator. "Boy, this heat has been wicked," he said. "What's for dinner? Roast chicken? Why in the world did you cook something that meant using the oven? That makes the kitchen even hotter. I should think you'd have had something you could cook on top of the stove."

Velma glared at him. "Well, pardon me," she said coldly. "How was I to know when I took that chicken out of the freezer this morning that it was going to be so beastly hot? You can be glad I bothered to cook at all."

"It smells great," Sven said hastily. "I only meant to be helpful. Where do you want to eat tonight? I'll set up."

"We'll eat on the deck," said Velma, mollified. "There's a little breeze out there. Call Lynette, will you?"

At the dinner table, Lynette picked at her food. She ate a few bites of chicken and a little rice, but didn't touch the carrots."

"Eat your carrots, Lynette," said Velma. "They are good for you."

"I don't want to. I hate carrots," said Lynette.

"I don't care if you hate them or not. If you hadn't eaten all those chips—" began Velma, but Sven interrupted.

"Aw, c'mon, honey, where is it written in stone that the kid has to like carrots? I didn't like them when I was a kid. She'll learn to eat more things when she grows up, but why try to make her eat something she hates?"

Velma shrugged, and said no more. Once the meal was over, she said to Sven, "Do you want to do dishes or give Lynette her bath and put her to bed?"

"I'll take care of the bath and bed detail," he said. "C'mon, sweetie, let's go plunk you in the tub."

This was one thing the little girl did not resist. She loved playing in the tub with her toys. The only thing she didn't like was having her hair washed, and Daddy never did that, only Mummy. Daddy let her play longer, too. Mummy was always in a rush. And she liked the way Daddy wrapped her in a big, fluffy towel to dry her off.

Going to bed was something else. She climbed in without any trouble, and Sven read her a story, but when he turned out the light, she protested. "I can't sleep yet, I'm not tired, it's too hot to sleep."

"Settle down," said Sven sternly. "It's important for little girls to get their beauty sleep." He went in the other room, where Velma was watching a sitcom on television.

In about two minutes, Lynette came into the room. "I can't sleep," she whined. "I want to watch television with you."

Her mother held out her arms. "Come sit on my lap," she said. "I haven't had a chance to hold you all day. It is hot in your room." Now it was Sven's turn to look angry, but he said nothing. After all, they had agreed that they wouldn't argue in front of Lynette.

So it went. Two parents who were always tired, and one very smart little girl who had learned just which buttons to push to get her own way.

Thursday night Velma met Sven with a serious look on her face. "Can you go to Lynette's school with me at eight o'clock tomorrow morning?" she asked. "Ms. Mancuso wants to talk to us. She says they are having a problem with Lynette."

"What kind of a problem?" he demanded. "They are supposed to know what they're doing. How much of a problem can a three year old girl be? Yeah, you bet I'll go. I want to know what this is all about."

"Don't lose your temper," Velma warned. "This is the best school we could find. They have a good reputation, and it's close to my job. I don't want them to kick her out."

Working together with the parents

The next morning Sven's truculence was softened by the director's friendly greeting. She thanked them for taking time to come in, and praised them for both coming. "It's so much better when both parents come to a conference," she said, and went on to talk about how hard it is when mother and father both work and have the responsibility of maintaining a home and trying to be good parents.

At this point they were ready to listen as Ms. Mancuso turned the meeting over to the teacher. Ms. Caporino spelled out in detail the difficulties she had been having, and the approach she was taking. "Lynette is a bright child, and she will learn how to get along in a group situation, but if we could work together, the process would be smoother. Could you tell me where she got the idea that she didn't have to do anything she didn't want to do? There are some rules all the children must obey."

Velma looked embarrassed. "I guess we gave her that idea," she admitted. "We read that parents aren't supposed to disagree in front of a child, so we let her get away with too much."

Agree on rules, then stick to them. Ms. Mancuso smiled. "It's true that parents need to be consistent about rules," she said, "but the important thing is that you two agree on the rules, then both stick to them. If one of you says 'No' and the other says 'Okay' that really gives mixed signals. Since you can't anticipate everything that will come up, one way to handle it is to question the child. If she comes to you with a request, Velma, ask her what her father said. If she admits that Daddy said 'No' then you smile and say pleasantly, 'Then that's the way it has to be.' And stick to it. Above all, don't be swayed by tears. The kind of tears that come because a child doesn't get her own way will not last if they are ignored."

"I hear you," Sven said and Velma nodded. "You're right. We will be more firm. From now on, we'll try to follow your advice."

"On my part, I'll try to ease up a bit," put in Gloria. "I guess maybe I've been a bit rigid, expecting Lynette to conform to our rules before she's had time to adjust to being in a group."

Ms. Mancuso stood and shook Sven's hand and then Velma's. "Now that we all understand the problem, let's give it a week and see what happens. You have a very smart little girl. If we follow a course of discipline that emphasizes sense, I'm sure Lynette will soon see the sense in acting in a way that brings approval and makes her feel good about herself."

Thanks to the director's prompt action and the willingness of parents and teacher to cooperate, this was one child who would not "slip through the cracks."

Highlights of Part One

Observation skills

Good observation skills are especially important with very young children who have not yet learned to express their feelings verbally. To understand when a child is showing signs of trouble, the adult needs to learn about the typical stages of development. A teacher who sees many children has a broad range of knowledge, while parents often have in-depth knowledge of their children. Adults need to be alert to the signals children give, and then react with sensitivity.

In the story about Joshua and Howie fighting, the teacher certainly knew Joshua was behind in learning to read, but was not as sensitive as she needed to be to the way the other children were teasing him and the growing resentment he harbored. In the story about Laura cheating, Charlene bent over backwards to be fair to her stepchildren and forgot to be sensitive to Laura's feelings.

Good communication

Communication is not just a matter of telling; it also means *listening*. Teachers must listen to parents, as well as talk to them, and vice versa. Teachers and parents expect children to listen to *them*, but do not always keep a receptive ear open for what the children have to say.

Teachers need to report to parents any changes in children's behavior or academic development. In addition, parents need to let teachers know about home situations that might affect a child's behavior in school.

Directors need to give the teachers any background information which might help them understand the children in their care. They also need to share their own knowledge of subjects which all their staff members may not have had a chance to learn. This falls under the heading of "staff training," which is another form of communication.

Follow-up is important

Whenever a problem is recognized and a plan is set up, there must be follow-up. Mrs. Rodriguez gave Tod's grandparents suggestions for them to follow; Fern Ellis outlined the steps she would take to help Penny and arranged to meet again with the grandmother; Norman Macrae kept in touch with Adam's parents and stepmother; and Mr. Riggs had follow-up meetings with the teachers and set up a series of meetings for parents. Only with good follow-up will you know if your plan is helping the child in question.

Bibliography for Part One

Books for children

Berman, Claire. (1982). *What Am I Doing in a Stepfamily?* Secaucus, NJ: Lyle Stuart.

Bradley, Buff. (1982). *Where Do I Belong? A Kids' Guide to Stepfamilies.* Reading, MA: Addison-Wesley.

Gardner, Richard A. (1982). *The Boys' and Girls' Book About Stepfamilies.* New York: Bantam Books.

Mayle, Peter. (1988). *Why Are We Getting a Divorce?* New York: Harmony House. Children fourth grade and up could read this book, but parents of younger children could use the language of the book to explain things to their children.

Prokop, Michael. (1986). *Divorce Happens to the Nicest Kids—A Self-Help Book for Kids.* Warren, OH: Alegra House.

Books for parents and teachers

Berman, Claire. (1986). *Making It As a Stepparent: New Roles/New Rules.* New York: Harper and Row.

Burns, Cherie. (1985). *Stepmotherhood: How to Survive Without Feeling Frustrated, Left Out or Wicked.* New York: Times Books.

Elkind, David. (1990). *Grandparenting: Understanding Today's Children*. Rosemont, NJ: Modern Learning Press.

Kalter, Neil. (1990). *Growing Up With Divorce*. New York: Free Press.

LeShan, Eda. (1993). *Grandparenting in a Changing World*. New York: Newmarket Press.

Rosen, Mark Bruce. (1987). *Stepfathering: Stepfathers' Advice on Creating a New Stepfamily*. New York: Simon and Schuster.

Magazine articles

Berman, Claire. "Stepparenting: How to Make It Work." *McCall's* v. 117, p. 97+, Nov. '89.

Fuller, Mary Lou. "Facts and Fictions About Stepfamilies." *The Education Digest* v.54, pp. 52-54, Oct. '88.

Kantrowitz, Barbara and Wingert, Pat. "Step by Step." *Newsweek* v. 114, Special Issue, pp. 24-25+, Winter '89/Spring '90.

Morgan, Amanda. "Happy Stepfamilies: What Are They Doing Right?" *Redbook* v.173, pp. 128-9+, May '89.

Rosen, Margery D. "Step-by-Step Parenthood." *Ladies Home Journal* v.109, p. 92+, Feb. '92.

Other resources

Stepfamily Association of America
215 Centennial Mall So. Suite 212
Lincoln, NE 68508

 ◆ Send for a catalog listing books for parents and children.

Grandparent Rights Organization
Suite 600, 555 So. Woodward Avenue
Birmingham, MI 48009

Grandparent Information Center
601 E Street, NW
Washington DC 20049

 ◆ Sponsored by the American Association of Retired
 Persons (AARP) and The Brookdale Foundation Group,
 the center provides resource information and referrals to
 local support groups for grandparents.

Grandparents Raising Grandchildren
PO Box 104
Calleyville, TX 76034

 ◆ For information about starting a group in your area, write
 to the address above. Enclose a SASE with double
 postage.

Inclusive
Education
&
Discipline

I NCLUDING CHILDREN WITH DISABILITIES in *all* schools, including private, independently owned preschools, was mandated by the Americans With Disabilities Act (ADA) in 1992. This act poses a challenge for directors, teachers and parents. In the past, owners of child care centers and nursery schools have been able to set their own restrictions. Many barred children who had a physical or cognitive disability that required extra time on the part of a teacher. They no longer have this choice. The Americans With Disabilities Act (ADA) applies to child care facilities as well as businesses. (Chapter 11 spells out the requirements of the ADA in more detail.)

When a director knows a child with a disability will be entering his or her school, it is up to the director to educate the staff about that particular problem. They need to know the functional and cognitive effects of that disability; what the child's capabilities are; and how the teacher can help that child be part of the regular class.

But it isn't only the children who have an adjustment to make. Teachers sometimes:

♦ Lack knowledge and experience in this area;

♦ Have preconceived ideas about how much the children can learn and how they will behave; and

♦ Feel uncomfortable in the presence of children who look or sound obviously "different" from the norm.

It takes time and a conscious effort to adjust these attitudes, but it *can* be done. There are child care centers and other preschool settings that have been successfully including differently-abled children for several decades now.

In Chapter 12, Grace Mitchell tells about her own growth in this area and describes some of the early efforts of her school, Green Acres.

When a child with paralyzed legs first enters a class, the teacher may see only the disability. Then a wonderful thing happens. As the teacher spends time with the child, the wheelchair fades into the background and the child emerges.

A good teacher wants *all* children to succeed, and has learned to focus on the strengths, not limitations of *all* children.

11

About Inclusive Education

Major require- ments of the Americans with Disabilities Act of 1992

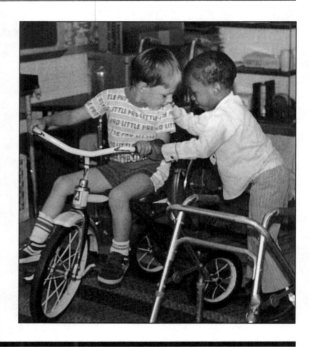

Long before the ADA, a series of Federal Laws were enacted to assure education for children and youth with disabilities. A major step toward that goal was the Education for All Handicapped Children Act of 1975, known as EHA. One provision of the EHA was:

> To financially assist the efforts of state and local governments in providing full educational opportunities to all children and youth with disabilities through the use of federal funds.

In 1990, Amendments to the EHA (P.L. 101-476), among other things, changed the name of the law to the Individuals with Disabilities Education Act (IDEA) and reauthorized federal funding.

PL99-457 was passed in 1986, mandating services to children at risk from birth to age five and to their families.

In order to receive federal funds, a state must develop a plan for providing for children with disabilities. These plans vary--some go *beyond* federal requirements. It is up to each director of each school to find out how much help is available in that state. A good place to start is with the director of Special Education in the local school system.

Highlights of the Americans with Disabilities Act (ADA) The movement toward Inclusive Education has been spurred on by the part of the Americans with Disabilities Act (ADA) that went into effect January 26, 1992, and included *day care centers*. The Public Accommodations requirements, as stated in the Americans with Disabilities Act Handbook (see Bibliography p. 150) include:

♦ **Integrated Settings**—A child cannot be excluded from regular activities. A center should plan and organize activities to include all children.

♦ **Elimination of Unnecessary Eligibility Criteria**—A child care center or family day home cannot impose rules that may screen out children with disabilities. A center is required to make changes in any policies which would deny enrollment to a child based on his or her disability.

♦ **Reasonable Modifications in Policies, Practices and Procedures**—A child care center or family day home is required to review its policies and make necessary changes in daily activities to include children with disabilities. However, if changes would affect the nature of the program dramatically, the change may not be required. Each child has different needs, and each change should be determined on an individual basis.

♦ **Removal of Architectural and Structural Communication Barriers**—Child care centers or family day homes are required to provide easy access to their facilities and activities for children with disabilities by removing obstacles, if doing so is "readily achievable."

♦ **Readily Achievable Alternative Measures**—If a center cannot easily remove an obstacle, it is required to use alternatives, if the alternatives are "readily achievable." Remember, alternative methods are only acceptable when removing an obstacle is not readily achievable.

♦ **Furnish Auxiliary Aids When Necessary**—A child care center or family day home is required to provide equally effective communication to children who have vision, hearing, speech or cognitive disabilities as to non-disabled children. If the center can show that providing a particular aid or service is very difficult or costly, the aid or service may be considered an "undue burden" and may not be required. Child care centers may not be required to purchase prescribed hearing aids or eyeglasses or perform services of a personal nature for children with disabilities, including assistance in eating, toileting or dressing.

♦ **Nondiscrimination Against an Individual Because of Known Association with a Person with a Disability**—A child care center cannot refuse to accept a child because the child knows or is related to a person with a disability. For example, a non-disabled child has a younger sister who is blind. The non-disabled child cannot be refused enrollment because of her sister's disability.

If you study the above requirements carefully, you will realize that they are not absolute. Do not jump to the conclusion that the ADA mandate will put you out of business if you are the owner of a small, private child care center, and cannot possibly afford expensive renovations.

Above all, we ask you to look at the purpose of the law—to open the doors to children who have previously been excluded, left "on the outside," because of disabilities. The very fact that there *are* child care centers that have been successfully including all children, even before the law took effect, shows that it can be done. Of course, passing a law does not mean instant change. The most important factor here is a change in *attitudes*, and that is always a slow process. In doing the research for this book, we have found a number of directors who honestly did not realize that anything about the ADA applied to them. Recognizing the law is the first step. Educating teachers about the various disabling conditions is the next. Such education should focus on what the child with a disability *can* do, as opposed to the sometimes frightening picture of what the child *cannot* do.

You may be a parent who has not realized what the law means to you. Before you rush out to the nearest child care center, look at the center carefully. Recognize that including a child with a disability may be a new experience for the school, one that is creating anxiety. Spend time with the director, and try to discern how he or she really feels about including children with disabilities. Is there wholehearted willingness, guarded acceptance, or downright reluctance? Who would your child's teacher be? Visit that class. Talk to the teacher. If you do not feel that your child would be happy in this setting, look at other centers. After all, the object is to make life better for the child.

12

"I found the courage to try what I thought was impossible."

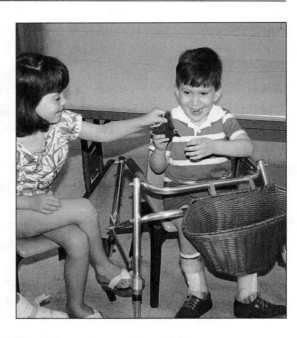

When the Americans with Disabilities Act was passed in 1992, some people in education rose up in horror, acting as if this were a brand new concept, dropped on them like an attack from outer space. As one of the matriarchs of child care, I offer my experience to put this act into historical context.

In the thirties, two children were enrolled in my private nursery school who, today, would be labeled "disabled." They happened to have the same name, so the children called them "big Jean" and "little Jean."

Big Jean was a beautiful child with chestnut curls and bright blue eyes. At the age of two she had suffered a serious illness and ran a high temperature which left her with brain damage. Physically she was tall and slim, but her bodily movements were erratic and unpredictable. Her speech was unclear, her voice shrill. When her parents took her out in public, she attracted attention, but in school she was simply accepted by the other children as one of them.

Little Jean was a child with Down Syndrome. Gentle and sweet, she was often chosen to be the baby in the housekeeping corner.

Both of these little girls came from homes where they were given a lot of love and attention. Their parents were grateful when I accepted them, which I could understand when I heard their tales of being cruelly rebuffed by other schools.

One day I was approached by a good friend who had helped me get my little school started. "Grace," she said, with a solemn expression, "I think you should know that some of the parents are upset because of those little girls who are obviously 'different.' Some parents are even threatening to take their children out."

I was surprised, shocked and apprehensive. It was during the great depression. My husband was out of work, and the modest tuition (I believe it was one dollar a week) was the sole support for my family.

"Thank you for telling me. I will have to think about it," I said.

I defined a clear entrance policy

After some real soul searching, I gave my answer. "As far as I am concerned all children have the same basic needs and the same rights. I will continue to accept enrollments on a first-come, first-served basis. Anyone who thinks their child will be harmed by this policy is welcome to spend a morning observing."

One mother accepted that invitation. Apparently, her report was favorable, because NOT ONE child was withdrawn.

Although I meant what I said, there were some children I thought we just could not accept. Then in the fifties, I attended a meeting of the Boston Association for Nursery Education where the speaker was Pauline Moore from the American Division for the Blind. She urged her listeners to include children who were blind.

Just that week I had turned away a four year old boy who had been blind from birth, explaining to his mother that our staff did not have the proper training to cope with his handicap. (We had not started using the terms "disability" or "differently-abled" then.) She pleaded with me to give him a chance, even offering to come with him.

"He wouldn't want me to hover over him," she said. "He is very independent, but I would be at hand if there were a problem, and I would be glad to volunteer my services in the office or wherever I could be useful."

I was adamant. "You can see that this is not like a school playground," I pointed out. "This is a farm, and the terrain is rough. I can't take the responsibility for your child's safety in this environment."

And then at the meeting I heard Pauline Moore say, "Your teachers do not have to be specially trained. These children do not need or want to be coddled. They are typical in every respect except their vision, and their greatest desire is to be treated like every other child. You need not fear for their safety. A child who is blind will not run in front of the swings. He probably will not run at all until he is very sure of himself."

Before I left that meeting, I assured the speaker that we would welcome at Green Acres a child who was blind, making a scholarship available if it was needed. The mother I had turned down was overjoyed when I called to tell her I had changed my mind.

I found the courage to try what I thought was impossible

It was at this point that my own growth took a giant step forward. By listening to another viewpoint, by believing what I heard, I found the courage to try, and to discover for myself that what I honestly had thought was impossible could indeed be done.

Shortly after that, three year old Joy came with her mother to visit. Joy was bubbly, outgoing and eager to try everything. It was clear that this mother was truly enjoying her little daughter, and for a number of years she lived up to her name and brought joy to all of us.

Joy was one of the many children who were blind who came to the Green Acres Day School, and even though they went on to the Perkins School for the Blind, they came back to us each summer for day camp. Everything Pauline Moore had promised proved to be true. We were constantly astounded by their ability to keep up with their peers in all aspects of the program. When nine year old Rusty, who was almost totally blind, hit the bull's eye in archery, the whole camp celebrated.

When the word got around, parents of children with other disabilities came, bearing tales of rejection and humiliation.

"I was made to feel guilty, as if I had committed a crime by bearing this child," one mother told me with tears in her eyes.

"I made an appointment, but when I arrived, the director took one look at Arnold and said coldly, 'There are places for children like that!' and shut the door in my face. I knew that if I told her on the phone that my child was disabled she wouldn't see us, but I thought she would feel differently when she saw him."

We learned from experience and used common sense

At Green Acres we were pioneers, venturing into unknown territory. There were no rules, no guidelines for including children who were handicapped in classes with "normal" children. We had to learn from experience and use our common sense.

I had to decide whether our program would be good for a particular child, and whether he would need so much time and attention that the rest of the children might be neglected.

I made the decision that my teachers would not be expected to lift a child or change the diapers of a three year old who was totally incontinent. Either a parent was there to help, or the parents paid for an aide.

I learned that the teachers had to be part of the decision. If they were apprehensive, they might be overly protective, which would deprive the child of the independence he or she needed. If they were turned off by a child's appearance, like Pearl, whose face was badly scarred from burns, the child's "radar system" would pick up the vibes.

Above all, if a teacher felt that an intolerable burden had been thrust upon him, I knew his or her resentment would stand in the way of success, and the child might feel at fault. Children with disabilities have enough to overcome without being made to feel that they have "failed."

Loving children was
not enough

A network of supportive professionals is essential. One of the most valuable but painful lessons I had to learn was that loving these children was not enough. We often worked with a doctor, psychologist or social worker who would be available to us on a continuing basis.

One terrible experience is still so vivid in my mind that it hurts when I dredge it up. In June, before the public schools closed, a school guidance counselor brought Dominic to me. The guidance counselor told me that he had been a behavior problem since his father had deserted the family. I couldn't believe this child, with his angelic smile and melting brown eyes, could be a problem. I soon learned he was a good actor.

"He desperately needs adult male supervision," she said. "Your counselors would be so good for him." We granted him a full scholarship.

By the third day after camp started, his counselors were up in arms. "That kid has the filthiest mouth I have ever heard," the unit leader reported. "He picks fights with the other kids, and for his size, he packs a mean punch. He refuses to participate in anything we do. He won't even put on his bathing suit when we go to the pool."

I called the school and found that the young woman who had brought him to us had left for the summer. We were on our own.

At least once a day he was back in my office, where he would be very contrite, promising to try harder.

"He is ruining the summer for the rest of the boys and for all of his counselors," was the next report. "I am afraid he will really hurt someone."

My husband and I took Dominic home. When we knocked, the door was opened by a sad, bedraggled woman with a baby on her hip.

"I'm sorry, but we can't keep Dominic," I said, and explained his behavior.

"I don't know what I'm gonna do with him. You can't kill 'em," was her glum answer.

The expression on Dominic's face and his mother's pathetic response are imprinted on my mind forever. Even as I write about it today I am grieving, wondering what else I could have done.

Learning is a two-way street

Over the years we enjoyed many bright, delightful youngsters who were challenged with almost every known disability. Having them in our midst was a two-way street—they gave us as much as they received.

Kathy was a four year old who was blind. She was eager to be involved in everything—very independent—hated to be taken by the hand and guided. I recall a day when a teacher brought me the following story. "We were down on the lower playground when I said that it was time to go in for juice. Stan jumped up and started off—you know Stan—he always has to be first. Suddenly he stopped short—went back to the sandbox where Kathy was seated, brushed the sand off her dress and walked beside her toward the building. He didn't hold her hand, but carried on a running conversation, letting his voice give her direction."

Developing compassion and understanding in children. A male counselor, with a touch of awe in his voice, described an equally touching event. "We were having a relay race," he said. "I noticed that Ricky *always placed himself opposite Alex, and then paced himself so Alex, a child partially disabled with cerebral palsy, was able to keep up. It was so subtle I thought I was imagining it until I saw it happen several times. These kids have more compassion and understanding than a lot of adults I know."*

Experiencing joy and satisfaction. Today the anxiety and fear that teachers have when children with disabilities are placed in their classes are the same feelings teachers at Green Acres felt, but it is just as true that those who open their minds and hearts and accept the challenge, feel the same joy and satisfaction we experienced fifty years ago.

13

He's very defiant and hard for teachers to manage.."

We were meeting over breakfast with a small group of parents who had agreed to share their experiences with us.

"My son Raymond is diagnosed with ADHD, Attention Deficit Hyperactivity Disorder," said Marilla. "He has a short attention span, can't focus on any one thing and doesn't listen, so he can't follow directions. His life has a lot of turmoil, because he can't control himself. He understands that, and he's sorry, but he just can't help it. He's very defiant, and hard for teachers to manage.

"At one preschool, he had a couple of care givers who weren't well trained. They didn't understand ADHD, and kept calling him a 'bad boy,' and making him sit in a corner. His self-esteem was driven lower and lower.

"One day when he was five, he asked me where babies come from. I explained to him about the sperm and the eggs. He's very bright, and I felt he could understand. Shortly after that, he had an especially hard day. When I was bathing him that night, he said to me in a contemplative way, 'You know, when your egg and Daddy's sperm got together, I think it was a bad mistake. I shouldn't have been born.' I could almost see the wheels turning in his head, and I knew what he was telling me. His struggle was so hard he couldn't deal with it."

"How did you deal with that?" Dr. Mitchell asked gently.

"I said, 'I'm really sorry you feel that way, because I love you very much, and I'm glad you were born,'" Marilla answered.

Be an advocate for your child. *This mother went on to tell us about her experience with public schools. Raymond is now in third grade. Each year she has gone in before school opened and explained the situation to the teacher and principal, showing them papers from the doctors to support her statements. Some teachers have responded sympathetically and have tried to be helpful. Others, she felt, just didn't believe Raymond was any different from any "bad boy."*

"How is Raymond's behavior at home?" we asked.

Concentrate on two or three major behaviors. *"At home, I adjust my thinking to his needs. I have a five year old daughter who does not have a problem. A friend came to visit with her two little girls. She thought it was terrible that I was more strict with Vivian than I was with Raymond. Vivian has to eat her vegetables. I don't even put vegetables on his plate. What they don't understand is that I concentrate on two or three major behaviors that need to be corrected and let the rest go. If I didn't do that, we'd be in constant conflict. Raymond wouldn't get any better, and I'd be a mess."*

ADD and ADHD are special problems

ADD and ADHD are comparatively new terms. There's a special problem in a situation like Raymond's. In the first place, ADD and ADHD (the H stands for Hyperactivity) are comparatively new terms. Many teachers have not learned what they mean and how to adjust their teaching to meet the needs of a child with this kind of a disability. Not only is the ADD and ADHD diagnosis frequently misunderstood, it is also mistaken for other disorders-emotional disturbance, behavior disorder or a learning disability.

Not all ADD and ADHD children are alike. Children with ADD have a short attention span and are unable to focus, so they can't follow directions. ADHD adds the factor of behavioral disorder. Not all children who have ADHD are alike. There is a range of 1-10. Johnnie, a child with ADHD, may only be diagnosed as a "2" and not present much of a problem. His teacher may wonder why another teacher is having such a hard time with Annie, who also has ADHD, not realizing that Annie is a "10" and much more disruptive.

The disability is not visible. Third, when a disability is not visibly apparent, it is much harder for people to admit it exists. Since this is a condition that manifests itself mainly in behavior problems, it is harder to decide whether the behavior is caused by the disability or is typical behavior for the age.

How can the school help?

Learn about ADHD. First, as with any other disability, both director and teachers need to learn as much as possible about the condition.

- Bring in a doctor (Raymond's doctor, if possible) or other related professional to explain what ADHD is, and how it affects children.

- The director could seek out an informative book, pick out the most important points, put them in layman's language and make copies for all the teachers.

- Invite Raymond's parents, and any others whose children have the same problem, to a staff meeting and give them a chance to share their experiences.

Concentrate on one or two major problems at a time. Second, like Raymond's mother, learn to concentrate on one or two major problems at a time. It is especially important not to make an issue of something that is done because "it has always been done that way," rather than because it is really necessary to health or safety.

Make adjustments as needed. Third, in making adjustments to meet the needs of a particular child, try to do it simply. You do not want to single out and embarrass the child with the disability.

One director's advice

The director of the preschool Raymond attended has a great deal of experience with this disorder and has learned all she can about it and how to deal with it. She offers the following advice.

Develop a specific management plan. It is extremely important to meet with the staff and discuss and develop a specific behavior management plan, and to communicate this plan to all the adults who will come in contact with this child.

Get professional help. In general, behavior management techniques that work well with regular kids do not work with ADHD kids. It is essential to get professional help from a psychologist or other behavioral specialist when creating a program for the child with ADHD, also keeping in mind the individual traits and needs of the particular child.

Firmness and consistency are important. Once a behavior management plan is developed, firmness and consistency are important. To do this, you must *make sure the child understands the consequences of behavior*. Perhaps even more important is stating the rules in a positive way, such as, "Keep your arms and your legs to yourself," instead of, "You may not hit or kick children!"

Be patient with yourself

Remember that a child, who is diagnosed as being in the upper range of ADHD may, like Raymond, know that he should not be doing something, but be unable to control himself. Acknowledge any effort. Reward the child for behaving in a positive way, whether or not compliance is with a target behavior. This is the catch "Catch them being good" strategy.

Do the best you can, but do not feel guilty or despairing if the changes you are hoping for are slow in coming. When you know you are doing your best, do not moan over the things that don't work, but celebrate every bit of success.

14

Clara

"I did it! I stood up by myself."

Four year old Clara frowned intently as she started the process her physical therapist had been teaching her. Sitting on the floor with her legs stretched out in front of her, she leaned forward and unlocked both braces at the knees. Next, she twisted her body so that she was in a kneeling position. She pulled her crutches to her, holding one on either side. Using the lower crossbar of the crutches to start with, she pulled herself up to a standing position. The last step was to lean down and relock her braces.

"I did it!" she cried triumphantly. "Look, Mr. Noonan, I stood up by myself." Her face was beaming with delight.

Mark Noonan and the children who had been watching clapped their hands and cheered. "Clara, that's wonderful," he managed to say over the lump in his throat. "Wait till I tell Ms. Pomerleau. She'll be so proud of you."

Mark thought back over the nine months Clara had been with them. This child had spina bifida. Both legs were paralyzed, but she had the use of her arms. When she first came to the center, she was dependent on others for almost everything. She spent all of her time in a stander or a wheelchair (with her braces unlocked at the knees so her legs could hang down). She was fearful of trying anything new, and too shy to respond to the friendly overtures of the other children.

One day a new person came to the school. Her name was Barbara Pomerleau, a physical therapist who had come to help Clara. In the months that followed, little by little, Clara mastered the use of crutches. At first Ms. Pomerleau walked behind her, holding her while she moved a few inches at a time. When Clara had learned to keep her balance while swinging her body forward as she shifted the crutches, Barbara encouraged her to try moving on her own. Again, she started by moving a few inches at a time, until eventually she could move about the room very confidently. It was necessary for Clara to be able to handle the crutches well before she could try the more complicated procedure of getting from the floor to a standing position. Today marked a real milestone in her progress.

Treating all children with respect

In education the goal is the same for all children. Over the years, Mark Noonan has worked with many children with special needs. His goal with Clara, as with other children, was to help her achieve more physical independence and to feel good about herself.

Mark worked in a school that had planned to include all children. He watched for opportunities to weave into the curriculum discussions of likenesses and differences. One day they might talk about the children's hair—brown, black, yellow, or maybe red; curly or straight; long or short. They were all different, yet they all had hair.

Another day he might concentrate on many ways they were all alike. They all had eyes, ears, a mouth, a nose. They all liked ice cream. They all liked to listen to stories.

Sometimes a child would ask a question. "Why does Clara have to wear those things on her legs? Don't they hurt? Does she have to wear them to bed? In the bathtub?"

Encourage children to talk openly and honestly about disabilities

Mark answered the first question calmly and openly. "Clara's muscles don't work like yours, so she has to learn other ways to manage. The braces help her to stand up straight. As for your other questions, why don't we let her answer. How about it, Clara? Do the braces hurt?"

Once their questions were answered, the children were satisfied and would go back to their activities.

There were things Clara could do. She could color and paint, make things with clay, build with table blocks and help stir the dough when the class made cookies. As her increased mobility gave her more confidence, she was ready to try other things and participate in the activities of the class.

Simple adaptations help

Sometimes simple adaptations can help in the goal of giving a child more independence. A small table with a rim to keep things from being knocked off by arms that work awkwardly; doing some activities on the floor; lowering an easel so a child can paint while sitting or kneeling on the floor.

Sometimes Mr. Noonan makes statements to acknowledge the feelings a child can't put into words.

"We all have trouble doing some things."

"When I first saw you, you couldn't walk on crutches. Look at you now."

"I know it's discouraging sometimes, but you are getting better."

Celebrate milestones, large and small

With some children, he has made a list of all the things that used to be hard and aren't any more.

Some children with disabilities show remarkable improvement with therapy and support, but it is important for both parents and teachers to recognize when a child has severe limitations. When this happens, you have to think in terms of SMALL STEPS, rejoicing over the tiniest gain.

No matter how limited the child is, you never stop trying. This dedicated teacher put it this way: "If you don't reach for the stars, you will never even get to the moon."

"Are those kids using sign language?"

"Good heavens!" exclaimed Paul Fabrizio. "Are those kids using sign language? They can't be more than two or three years old. Is someone in that group deaf?"

Mr. Fabrizio was considering entering his son in this child care center in Massachusetts, and the director, Ms. Perlman, was showing him around. She smiled at his surprise.

"Yes, that is sign language, and no, no one is deaf in that class. However, Quentin, that little redhead with the freckles, does have some loss of hearing

---

and a severe speech impairment. Because the children find it hard to understand him, he sometimes uses sign language, so Ms. Morisette has taught them how to "read" his signals, and respond. They also talk to him, because he can hear them. You see, when Quentin was between the ages of 18 and 30 months, he had a number of ear infections, and he missed out on the normal stages of language development. He didn't hear the words being spoken, so they didn't become part of his vocabulary. Now he has some hearing, BUT he does not hear the same sounds the others hear, so his speech is not clear, although it is gradually improving."

"Boy, that must be awfully hard for a little kid to handle," said Paul.

"Oh, it is," affirmed Ms. Perlman. "He's very cheerful and happy now, but when he first came to us about eight months ago, he had some real behavior problems. He grabbed things from children, and hit or kicked them if they did not respond when he tried to talk to them. We are fortunate enough to have our own special education teacher, and she worked with Ms. Morisette to develop a plan for Quentin. Also, as part of his IEP, a speech therapist comes here and works with him twice a week. She helped both the teacher and the other children learn how to "sign."

Paul frowned. "This is great for Quentin, but the teacher must have to spend a lot of time with him. What about the other kids? Don't they miss out? Or does she have an aide?"

"There is an aide whose time is shared with two other teachers, and that helps. However, I think Alena Morissette would have managed even without an aide. She began by talking to the other children, explaining that she needed to help Quentin learn to speak better and asking them to help her.

"They loved learning how to 'sign.' It's like a new game to them, and personally, I think it's a good thing for everyone to know.

"Each day she helps all the other children get started on their own activities, then she works with Quentin. She sits down and looks right into his face when *she talks to him. I never hear her raise her voice, but she speaks slowly and distinctly. She often uses hand gestures to help communicate her meaning. She waits for him to answer, and repeats words he is not saying correctly. When he doesn't seem to understand something, she "signs" it for him. At the same time, she keeps an eye on the others, and is ready to help if they need her.*

"Children are so quick to copy what adults do—they watch Ms. Morisette, and I see them move so they can look directly at Quentin when they want to talk to him. It's wonderful to see how his whole attitude has changed. He doesn't have to 'act out' his frustration."

Paul Fabrizio shook his head in amazement and admiration. "I'm glad that my son doesn't have a problem like that, but watching you and your teachers with Quentin has convinced me that this is the place for Enrico."

What are the warning signs of a possible hearing problem?

We were able to talk at some length with the special education teacher in that child care center. She had previously taught for six years with a certified teacher for the deaf, and had brought the knowledge she gained to this new position.

Frequent or persistent ear infections. A child can be on antibiotics for eight months or more before an infection clears up. In addition, it can take up to six weeks after an infection clears for hearing to return to normal.

Uncontrollable behavior. Let's say Mr. and Mrs. Brown have a three year old daughter who has a constant behavior problem. She hits her two year old brother and grabs things from him, she punches and kicks her parents—they don't know how to control her. They decide to send her to preschool, honestly admitting to the director that they don't know what to do and hope the teachers will know how to "make her behave."

The Browns are lucky. This school, as part of its enrollment procedure, has a detailed health form. It asks, "Has this child ever had ear infections? At what age? How often?" Their answers prompt the school to recommend a hearing examination, where it is discovered that their daughter has a partial hearing loss.

The Browns are relieved to know there is a physical reason which may cause for the bad behavior. They now understand that their daughter's behavior stemmed from her frustration.

Persistent "baby talk." Sometimes the parents of a three year old who doesn't speak clearly might think the child just hasn't outgrown "baby talk," but *any* time a child has a speech problem, hearing should be checked, and especially if there is a history of ear infections. As Quentin's story shows, there are ways to help the child learn to communicate with others, and to become part of the world around him.

How can the teacher help?

Help the child become part of the class. Alena Morisette had not had any previous experience working with children who have hearing impairment and speech difficulties. She concentrated on helping Quentin become part of the class, improving his ability to communicate with the others and feeling good about himself. As she did these things, she was providing a strong role model for the other children.

All children need special care. Both the special education teacher and the director stressed that this kind of caring and planning was not kept in reserve for children with disabilities. They may not always be as obvious, but *every* child has a need. Angus may have a temper; Maralee may be extremely shy; Gregory may be unable to cope with teasing; Olive may be clumsy and awkward, always knocking things over.

A good teacher watches the children's interactions. He or she listens to voices, both the tones and the words. The teacher makes each child feel special and important. It is not easy, but then, a teacher like Ms. Morisette does not have to spend much time and energy scolding and breaking up fights.

16

Kyle-Michael

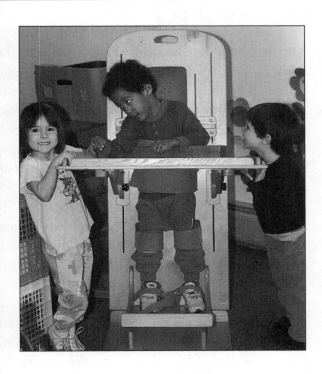

"Two buddies come over, put an arm around him and press a cheek against his."

Let me tell you about Kyle-Michael. He is almost four years old. He has black, curly hair and an enchanting smile. He also has cerebral palsy, which in his case has caused quadraparesis, a condition which weakens the muscles of all four limbs. He cannot walk. He cannot use his arms, though he can grasp something in his right hand and get it into his mouth. His neck muscles are not strong, so he has trouble holding his head up, and usually his upper body leans to one side.

He also attends a preschool in New England, where he has many friends. His teacher, Lisa; his specialists; the other children; and Joanne, his full-time aide, are all his friends. When Kyle-Michael first arrives in the morning, Joanne helps him into his custom-made, high-tech stroller. The wide plastic tray she attaches at chest level helps Kyle-Michael to stay upright. He sits in this while Lisa reads a story to all the children.

After the story, the others move to different areas of the room for a variety of activities. Joanne lifts Kyle-Michael out of the stroller, sits on the floor with him on her lap, and massages his feet and ankles. She is relaxing his muscles so she can fit his feet into the foot braces. They look like clear plastic shoes, low in the front, high in the back. He needs them to brace his legs in the "stander." This is a board as tall as Kyle-Michael. Joanne fastens him to the board with straps around his legs, below and above the knees, and attaches a wooden tray. She tilts him back so she can wheel him over to a table where several children have set out toy dishes and plastic food. (The wheels can only be used when the "stander" is tilted, so it cannot roll when he is standing in it.) One little girl puts a piece of rubber "pizza" in his mouth, and he bites down on it. Joanne takes it away, saying, "Come on, Kyle-Michael, you know that's only make-believe," and he grins at her mischievously.

Just then a new person arrives on the scene, a smiling woman with a carton full of toys. This is Dr. Betsy Gibbs, Preschool Coordinator and Educational Consultant in the town where Kyle-Michael lives. The toys in her carton are all made so children with limited use of their hands and/or arms can play with them. They work by pressing buttons or switches. She is returning them from a meeting the night before where they were shown and explained to parents. These expensive toys would not be within the budget of most child care centers, but they are provided by state funds to meet Kyle-Michael's needs. Dr. Gibbs puts them on a low table and the children gather around with excitement as she passes them out. Obviously, this is something they have done before and enjoyed. The one she puts on Kyle-Michael's tray is a tape recorder which he can play by pressing a plastic circle about four inches in diameter. "Here's your music, Kyle-Michael," she says cheerfully.

His face lights up and he reaches out eagerly to press the circle. A catchy song fills the air, and his head and shoulders start moving to the music. He is holding his head up straight. When his hand slips off the button, the music stops and he cries, "More!"

"You want more music, Kyle-Michael? Press the button. You can do it."

These toys, used by Kyle-Michael and the other children, are one way Kyle-Michael becomes part of the group. He is doing what the others are doing.

Two boys are his special "buddies." *Perhaps, at first, the children were curious about the special chair, the foot braces and straps and stander, but it is clear that they now see him as one of them. Sometimes he has to be helped, and they do this calmly and simply, almost automatically. Different children come over to show him what they are making. Two boys are his special "buddies," and will come over, put an arm around him, press a cheek against his.*

At snack time, Kyle-Michael says, "Bagel," his eyes lighting up.

"That's right, we are having bagels today," says Joanne, and breaks off a piece and puts it in his hand. With some effort, he gets the morsel into his mouth and starts chewing.

Kyle-Michael has developed a vocabulary of about fifty words. He repeats words after Lisa or Joanne or one of the children. He has not yet started using phrases, but his teachers feel that he will. Yet his parents were told that he would never talk!

Kyle-Michael has friends, he is learning, he belongs! With the help of several different specialists, he is developing new skills. He really is a happy little boy!

Treat him as a child, first

The worries I have heard expressed by teachers aren't always about putting on braces, helping a child eat, building ramps and widening bathroom doors. Often they are about the "D" word—Discipline. "How do you discipline a child who's paralyzed? Whose face is scarred from terrible burns? Who has a terminal illness? Who can't see? Can't hear? Can't talk? I couldn't scold the poor kid; hasn't life been hard enough on him?"

The key lies in those words, "the poor kid." As long as you think of a child that way, you can neither discipline him nor help him. Neither can you assume that because life has treated him badly he is going to "get even" by making it hard for you. If he talks back, hits someone, uses bad language or in other ways behaves unacceptably, treat him as you would any other child of that age. Look for reasons, not in the disability, but in what is happening right then and there. Is the way he is behaving to be expected of any four year old in that same situation?

How would you discipline another child, a "typical" child?

Remember, any discipline that is inappropriate for a "typical" child is inappropriate for a child with a disability.

Do teachers need special training?

What about Lisa, his teacher? Had she had training in working with children with CP, or any other disability? Was she frightened or overwhelmed by the thought of having a child with multiple disabilities in her class? No. She said frankly that when Kyle-Michael first came, she knew nothing about his cerebral palsy or quadraparesis, but she set about to learn all she could, from reading, from listening and from observing the specialists who came in.

Although Joanne usually takes care of Kyle-Michael, Lisa has learned to do everything he needs. What is most important is that she knows children, and she sees him as a child and treats him as she does all the other children in her class. She knows that what he needs most are love and acceptance, and those she gives him in abundance.

Author's note

The names in this chapter are real. At the time this visit took place, Kyle-Michael attended the Newport PreSchool in Newport, New Hampshire. According to director Karen Dewey, Kyle-Michael's parents were proud and pleased to think his story might help teachers everywhere to see children with disabilities in a different light. Lisa, the teacher; Joanne, the aide; and Dr. Gibbs all shared that feeling.

17

Ada

"I knew I wasn't dumb. I wanted to read."

How does it feel to have a learning disability?

Today we read about the problems of a child with a learning disability, and we speculate about that child's feelings, and we try to help—but we can't really know how it feels. It seemed to us worthwhile to hear, from someone who went through this pain, how it really was.

"It began with the alphabet. All the other children knew the alphabet long before I could say the letters and recognize them. I think I was in second or third grade before all those lines on paper meant anything to me. Then I couldn't understand why the teacher would hold up a picture with the letters that made the name of that picture, and say it backward. Like, she would hold up a picture of a cat, and say C-A-T, when I could plainly see that it said T-A-C.

"I knew I wasn't dumb. My mother was in an accident when I was eight and became crippled. My older sister was deaf and losing her sight. My father went away for weeks at a time. So, at eight, I became mother of the family. I cooked and cleaned and carried clothes to the neighborhood laundry. I was big and strong for my age, so I could go to the grocery and offer to sweep and clean up the store in return for food. I could do all that, so I didn't feel dumb—except at school. I couldn't read, and I didn't know why!

"I hated school. Every year it got worse, because there were more and more things to learn, and all of them took reading. And nobody listened when I said I couldn't read. So many times a teacher said to me, 'You could do it if you tried,' or 'You're just too lazy to try.'

"They kept moving me up in the grades, even though I couldn't do the work. I guess it was because I was so big. What I hated most was when the teacher called on all the children to read part of a story. When it was my turn, I didn't even know where they were in the book, much less know what the words said. Then the teacher would hit me across the knuckles with a ruler, and boy, that hurt! One day I grabbed the ruler and broke it. I told her if she ever hit me again I'd hit her right back—but she did, and I did. She sent me to the office, and the next thing I knew, they sent me to a different school. It was a lot farther away, and I didn't have money for street cars, so I had to start extra early so I could walk."

"I knew I wasn't dumb. I wanted to read."

We were listening to Ada, a woman of seventy. She was talking about the early thirties, the depression years, in New York City. Teachers were undertrained, overworked and the word "dyslexia" had never been heard of.

"How did you overcome this?" asked Grace. "I know you can read now, and you ran your own business successfully. How?"

Ada smiled. "It was several things," she said. "First of all, I wanted to read. I envied the people who could pick up a book or a magazine and read it with ease. Second, I knew I was smart about a lot of things. Third, I learned how to cover up.

"Over the years in school, I had picked up some things. I knew the sounds the letters made. I could recognize small words that you see over and over, but long ones were just a jumble. I fixed myself a piece of cardboard with a slot just big enough for me to see about four letters at a time. I would slide that along, working out the sounds and saying them aloud, until suddenly I would hear them and recognize the word. Once I figured out one of those words, I would know it the next time I saw it. Sometimes I could get the meaning of a word by looking at the whole sentence. If I read, 'The man fell into the water and he couldn't swim, so he dr_____' I could guess that the word was 'drowned.'

My goal was to read ten minutes a day

"I set myself a goal to read ten minutes every day. This was late at night after I had gotten my mother and sister to bed and finished the work. Gradually, I worked up to an hour a day, and I still read an hour every day. Only now I can read a lot more in an hour.

"As for covering up, I was ashamed to let anyone know I couldn't read like other people did. When I had my own business, if someone brought me a piece of paper and said, 'Will you read this and see if it's OK?' I would say, 'I'm in the middle of something important right now. Come back in an hour.' Then I would lock myself in the rest room and figure it out.

"I never knew till I was an adult what was wrong with me. One day a woman who taught in a local college came to spend some time looking at my counseling business. When she was ready to go, she said, 'I congratulate you. You handle your LD very well.'

'What do you mean?' I asked. 'Your learning disability,' she said, and then explained what dyslexia is.

"After all these years I had an answer to that why, a reason for all the struggles. Here was a woman who knew about me and she wasn't laughing at me or looking at me with scorn. You can't imagine what that meant to me.

"Today, thank God, it is better for children. It isn't easy, but teachers are trained to recognize the problem, and help the kids so they don't grow up wondering why, why, why?"

How can parents and teachers help children with learning disabilities?

Screening programs. Today the picture is much brighter for children like Ada. Public schools have programs where qualified examiners screen children for learning disabilities. Once identified, IEP's (Individual Education Plans) are set up to help these children. The IEP is created by a team which includes the parent and teacher;. the IEP outline all needs and identifies what educational interventions are to be part of the school program for the child. Classroom teachers have more training in working with IEP's, and specialists supplement what is done in the classroom. Parents are involved, and helped to understand what they can do at home.

Preschool programs such as Head Start have done a great deal to identify symptoms which may be diagnosed later as a learning disability.

The director has the primary responsibility. In all daycare or child care facilities it is the primary responsibility of the director to obtain the training to work with children like Ada. The director must learn as much as possible about the topic and then pass the knowledge on to the staff. The director also needs to know what resources are available to the child, the teachers and parents. The local school department usually has this information.

Coordination between professionals and teachers. Since children who are not yet in public school will, at best, probably be seen only once or twice a week by a specialist, child care teachers need to know as much as they can in order to work in partnership with other professionals.

18

Donny

"I'm tired of being the good one!"

"Donny, I have a lot of papers to correct tonight. The baby's clothes are in the dryer. Will you please take them out, fold them and put them in her room?" Sheila Carney was already spreading papers out on the just-cleared dining room table, and not really looking at her middle son as she spoke, so it was a shock when she heard an explosive, "NO!"

"What did you say?" she gasped, dumbfounded. Was this the Donny who had always been the most helpful of her three boys?

All of them had done their homework in the afternoon so they could watch television after supper, and that's what they were doing.

"Why do I have to do it?" Donny shouted angrily. "I want to watch television just as much as they do. You never ask them to do anything! It's always, 'Donny, do this!' and 'Donny, do that!' Well, I'm sick and tired of being the good one!"

Sheila's immediate reaction was to protest that it wasn't true. She treated them all the same they all had to help. But her mind was racing, and she realized that he was right.

Sheila's little girl, Donna, came along seven years after the boys. At three she was a beautiful, happy and loving child; all her brothers adored her and were proud of her. BUT it was Donny who, from the very beginning, had been most willing to take care of her. He fed her, rocked her and even changed her diapers—a chore her other brothers dodged.

Was she exploiting his good nature?

It wasn't just in taking care of Donna. He helped Sheila in many ways, she realized. Her marriage had ended in divorce when Donna was two. Donny seemed to understand how hard it was for her to teach school, take care of a big house and be mother and father to four children. Often when she dragged home exhausted, Donny would be ironing or running the vacuum. His brothers gave her arguments; he always did what she asked of him. Was I really exploiting his good nature? she wondered. Yes, she realized with guilt. The rest were "getting away with murder," because she was taking the easy way out.

Admit you've made a mistake

Sheila took a deep breath. "You are right, Donny. I hate to admit it, but I have been taking advantage of you! I'm really sorry, and from now on, things are going to be different. Come on, boys, turn off that television! You are all going to help, and when the work is done, you can all watch your programs. Understood?"

Donny's angry look faded, and he came over and gave Sheila a hug. She had to learn a hard lesson through her own mistakes.

Expecting too much from other children in the family

This true story was offered to a group of young mothers, each of whom had a child with a disability. A common problem seemed to be that they were expecting too much of the other children in the family. Several had stories to share.

Trisha had an eight year old son with cerebral palsy. She said, "Often I let him get away with things that I don't let his sisters do."

"How do your other children feel about this?" someone asked.

Talk with the other children about the disability

"They resented it until I sat down with them alone and explained why. Now it is better; in fact, they are pretty good about it. But I am concerned about Lana. She is the oldest, she is twelve. She's very motherly with my son. She helps me a great deal, with him and with my younger daughter, Julie. Julie is a mischief-maker, and when she gets into something, my husband will yell, 'Lana, get your sister.' He never yells at me, it's always Lana. He knows I might yell right back at him."

Keep demands reasonable

Another mother, Ginny, said, "I was divorced, and I married Hank when Graham was two. He is seventeen now, and Hank and I have two other boys, ten and four. Graham grew up thinking of Hank as his father. Our middle child is on the border of ADD, and I have to give him special attention. That's stressful for the rest of the family. We put a lot of pressure on the big guy because he's the oldest. We tell him, 'We expect more of you because you're the biggest.' We think we're being reasonable, but relatives tell us we're not."

The true story about Donny points up the fact that this kind of a problem can develop in *any* family, not just those that include a child with a disability. However, the parents we have talked to seem to indicate that it almost "goes with the territory" when one child needs more attention than the others. It's easy for a parent to fall into the trap of exploiting the willing child, but if you do this, you may well be brought up short when that 'good' child runs out of patience and explodes one day. Then it is up to you to take a hard look at things and bring them back into balance.

19

Annette

"Maybe I'm not the right person to work with a child with cerebral palsy."

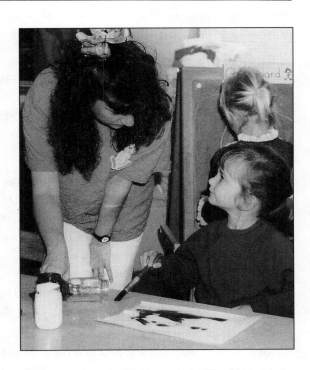

"Oh, Annette, not again!" exclaimed Carol with a mixture of dismay and exasperation. The curly-headed five year old looked up at her with a mischievous grin, as the water she had just spilled spread around her. Carol went to the sink for a sponge, mopped up the spilled water, and lifted Annette out of her chair. "No more painting today," she said firmly. "Why don't you go play with something else?"

Annette looked up with tear-filled eyes, sat down on the floor and began to sob.

"Don't cry, sweetheart," said Carol, stricken with guilt. "I didn't mean to scold you. Here, let's go over to the doll corner and you can rock the doll in the cradle." She helped Annette to her feet, and took her hand as the child moved awkwardly across the room. The teacher stayed with her until she seemed to be happily settled with a doll.

What is it like working with a child with cerebral palsy?

That afternoon, while the children were napping, Carol asked to speak to her director, Mrs. Dawson. "Maybe I'm just not the right one to work with a child with cerebral palsy," she said unhappily, after telling what had happened. "I've tried to be patient, but after she spilled the painting water three times, that was it. I just don't want her to paint any more."

Mrs. Dawson shook her head, even as she smiled sympathetically. "That's not the answer," she said firmly. "She loves to paint, and we won't take that away from her. However, I think the fault is more mine than yours. When Annette's regular teacher broke her hip and you came in to fill her place, I didn't spend enough time with you. At the beginning of the year, Annette's mother came in and talked to all of us about working with a child with a disability, cerebral palsy in particular. I think I'll ask her to come in again. She has made it her business to learn all she can about CP and how it affects her daughter's ability to learn. In the process she has also learned a great deal about including children with special needs in a regular classroom. It will be much better for you to hear from her directly, than second-hand from me."

The next day, Ms. Grant-Winter rearranged her schedule so she could leave work and come to the school in the afternoon. She greeted Carol with a warm smile, and seemed to understand her feeling of uncertainty.

Is the disability the cause of the misbehavior or is it something else?

Good communication is essential. *"Tell me what happened," she said, and when Carol described the episode, she nodded. "You say she looked up at you with a 'mischievous grin,' and that's a key. When Annette behaves in a way that isn't acceptable, I have to ask myself whether it is because of her CP or the naughty behavior of a 'typical' five year old. Let me tell you what I would have done. The first time she spilled the water, I would have mopped it up, as you did. However, if it happened again, and if she looked at me with a grin and a devilish gleam in her eye, I would have asked her, 'Are you tired? Do you want to stop painting?' If she said yes, then I would have cleaned up and moved her to something else. I want her to communicate verbally, so I would have said something like, 'Thank you for telling me that. It is good when you tell me how you feel, but spilling the water wasn't the best way to let me know you wanted to stop.' Then I would have tried to model a better way for her. If she said no, then I would have asked, 'Are you just being naughty?' Surprisingly, she will often say yes. Then I would say, 'Well, this is good communication. Thank you for telling me you're being naughty, but we have rules. One of the rules is, you can't just knock over the water for the fun of it. If you want to try blocks where you can knock things over, I'll help you out of the chair so you can move over there, but just because you think this would be fun doesn't mean you can do it.'"*

"That's wonderful!" exclaimed Carol.

What does this child's misbehavior mean?

Use an internal checklist. *Ms. Grant-Winter looked at her directly. "The important thing is, you use an internal checklist with any child whose behavior is unacceptable. It is a list of questions you ask yourself to decide what the* behavior means. In Annette's case, you fine tune that checklist. You ask 'Is she just bored and being mischievous? Or is it because of the CP that she cannot grasp the cup and hold it steady?' By the way, Annette's other teacher came up with an idea that helped in painting. She cemented a cup to a wider base of kitchen tile, so it couldn't tip over easily."

"I saw that in the closet," said Carol. "I just didn't realize what it was for. Perhaps I can find some other ways to help Annette to learn."

Arranging flexible classrooms such as multi-age groupings

Teachers must be willing to accept a child with a disability being assigned to them. This can be a major sticking point, but one director solved it with multi-age classrooms. Instead of a class for threes, one for fours and one for fives, she regrouped the children into three classes, each of which combined all three ages. That meant that a child at any of those age levels could be placed with any one of three teachers. The teacher who just wasn't ready to work with a particular child wouldn't have it forced on him or her.

There are other advantages to this kind of grouping. A five year old child who is developmentally at age three can be in the group, and so can the three year old who is ready to be with the fours. The teacher is the one who has to be flexible in planning and thinking.

In some states, among them Minnesota, Michigan and Kansas, the majority of child care centers have mixed age grouping. In Minnesota, child care centers almost never separate threes, fours and fives, arguing that there can be a difference between the chronological ages and maturity levels of those children. However, they would not be allowed, by state law, to include twos with threes or older.

Matching expectations of both parents and schools

The director of a private school in Massachusetts feels that an important key is applying the same entrance requirements to all children, regardless of their abilities. She said, "I have an initial interview with every parent who enrolls a child. I ask them what they are looking for and what they want and expect the school to do for their child. Every parent has certain expectations. Then I tell them whether our school can meet their wishes, and in what ways we cannot. It is not always a disability that prevents a good match. A parent may have strong feelings about discipline. When I was told by a father that if his son misbehaved I was to spank him, I replied firmly that such an action was against our policies. That father chose not to enroll his child in my school. I would not refuse to take a child with a disability, but if it is clear to the parent and to me that our school is not the best place for the child, they are usually ready to look elsewhere."

Communicate with all parents early in the school year. When we asked this same director if there was a problem with the other parents, she agreed that there could be, but felt there didn't need to be if the school did some careful preparation. When they knew a child with a disability was going to enroll in September, the staff sat down, discussed it and made some careful plans. About two weeks after school began, they sent home a brochure about *all* the children. They put in pictures and gave a little information about each child, emphasizing the positive. This gave parents an introduction to all the children, including the one with the disability, and an opening to ask questions if they wanted to. About a week later the teachers called each parent, to say, "Our school year is under way, and I wanted to tell you about some of the things your child is doing and give you a chance to ask any questions you might have." At this time there were some questions about the child with the disability, but no one suggested that he shouldn't be there.

Keep parents involved and informed. An owner/director from Cape Cod has, from the time she first opened, accepted all children, BUT she requires all parents to be closely involved. That doesn't mean they have to go on field trips or volunteer in the classroom. It does mean that they have to keep in close touch with the school, be willing to come in if there is a problem, and help find a solution to that problem.

Finally, a quote from another director. "We look for teachers who want to grow, are willing to change, are challenged and stimulated rather than overwhelmed by the thought of working with special needs children."

General Guidelines for Inclusive Education

The following suggestions were made by Ms. Grant-Winter:

Children need to misbehave

All children, including those with disabilities, need to misbehave sometimes. It's a normal part of child development. However, a child with a disability may have a limited number of ways to misbehave. For example, a five year old girl in a wheelchair who can only move her head back and forth can't have a tantrum, so she may spit out her food.

Teachers must be willing

If it is at all possible, do not put a child with a disability with a teacher who is unwilling or feels unable to cope. Some teachers resent being asked to accompany a five year old to the bathroom to help remove braces. On the other hand, there are practical things to make everyone's life easier. For example, underpants with velcro tabs, so braces don't have to be removed every time a child goes to the bathroom.

Directors should know of resources available

It is up to the director of the school to investigate the resources within the community and discover what is available. This may be done through the public school system, pediatricians or local hospitals. Also research what each state has to offer.

Many children are identified through the local public school system Child-Find Identification Process, and the first suggestion is usually Early Intervention, but parents need to know they have a range of options. They can go to a pediatrician, or they can look for services at a hospital or a clinic. In some states there are Developmental Disability Evaluation Clinics, usually associated with a large hospital.

Developmental pediatricians

Not all pediatricians understand the needs of children with disabilities. A developmental pediatrician, often associated with a hospital Special Needs Clinic, specializes in anything that could delay normal development in young children.

Collaboration is the key

Once a child is diagnosed, deciding how best to help that child demands a team effort. Teacher, director, parents and specialists need to meet and work together. To help them over rough spots, parents may have developed a "bag of tricks" which they can share with the teacher. As for the teacher, because she sees many children, she can often reassure the parents that a certain behavior is normal. For example, during the last week of school, Annette became more and more difficult. The night before the final day she cried, then got really wild. I thought it was the CP that made Annette unable to face change, but the teacher assured me that many children Annette's age react that way. Hearing the words "last day" and "last time" is very frightening to them. They don't know what is going to happen to them.

Of course, when something happens that neither the parent, the teacher or the director knows how to handle, they will look to the specialists for help.

Parents need time

It's very important that all members of the team understand that after a diagnosis or a referral it takes parents time to digest the information. It may take a week, a month or even longer. They may want a second, or even a third opinion, and just getting appointments can take a month or more.

No matter what the "experts" recommend, the final decision on the child's program rests with the parents, and the teacher must accept and support that decision.

Terminology is important

It is important to *use words that put the child before the disability.* Say "a child with a hearing impairment," or even "a child who is deaf," not "a deaf child"; "a child with an emotional disability," not "an emotionally disabled child." It is a subtle point, but it keeps adults from letting a child's disability become his or her label.

Educate the other children

Sometimes you have to educate the other children and give them tools to respond to a child who may be unintentionally hurting them. For example, Annette has trouble grading hand movements, that is, discerning how hard she is touching someone. If she seems to be hitting when she is trying to touch another child, that child should not just say, "Stop it!" but, "Annette, I know you're trying to get my attention, but please do it in a gentle way." Even when she was three, the other children in her room learned to do this because the teacher modeled it for them. She also modeled for Annette. If a child jostled her, Annette learned to say "No!" without getting angry, and the child learned, "I can't jostle Annette because she has a little trouble walking."

Don't panic

Do not assume you will be facing the worst possible situation. Schools have included children with a wide range of learning capacities and emotional behavior for many years. Children with *severe* physical or medical disabilities make up a small part of the population.

Benefits of inclusion

People tend to think that it is the child with a disability who benefits in an inclusive classroom, but for the other children, there are also huge advantages. Children in various stages of normal development benefit:

♦ by learning that there are many different kinds of people in the world, and "different" doesn't mean "bad";

♦ from a lower student-teacher ratio (if there is an aide);

- from the extra time and care the teacher puts into planning;

- from the specialists who often include all the children in the projects they have planned for the child with the disability. (Annette's teacher says they do projects in that class they would never have done if Annette and her specialist had not been there.) Among the specialists who might come into the classroom are an occupational therapist, a mobility therapist, a speech and language pathologist or a psychologist; and

- from learning by a variety of adapted techniques and pieces of equipment which makes learning activities more varied and less routine.

- by developing better thinking and problem-solving skills. This happens when a good teacher involves *all* the children in figuring out how one child's needs can be met.

Bibliography for Part Two

Books for children

Bahan, Ben and Dannis, Joe. (1987). *Signs for Me: Basic Sign Language for Children*. San Diego, CA: Dawn Sign.

Bunnett, Rochelle. (1993). *Friends in the Park*. New York: Checkerboard Press.

Cairo, Jasmine and Shelley, Tara. (1985). *Our Brother Has Down's Syndrome*. Toronto, Canada: Annick-Firefly Books Ltd.

Dwight, Laura. (1992). *We Can Do It*. New York: Checkerboard Press.

Dyer, T.A. (1990). *A Way of His Own*. Boston: Houghton Mifflin.

Lasker, Joe. (1980). *Nick Joins In*. Morton Grove, IL: Whitman.

Powers, Mary. (1986). *Our Teacher's in a Wheelchair*. Morton Grove, IL: Whitman.

Wright, Betty. (1981). *My Sister Is Different*. Chatham, NJ: Raintree-Steck Vaughan Publishers.

Books for parents and teachers

Allen, K. Eileen. (1991). *The Exceptional Child— Mainstreaming in American Education*. Ventura, CA: Delmar.

Bergman, Thomas. (1976). *Seeing in Special Ways: Children With Blindness*. Milwaukee, WI: Gareth Stevens.

Bergman, Thomas. (1989). *Finding a Common Language: Children Living With Deafness*. Milwaukee, WI: Gareth Stevens.

Bergman, Thomas. (1989). *On Our Own Terms: Children Living With Physical Disabilities*. Milwaukee, WI: Gareth Stevens.

Bergman, Thomas. (1991). *Going Places: Children Living With Cerebral Palsy*. Milwaukee, WI: Gareth Stevens.

The above books are part of a series with text and photographs by Thomas Bergman. Written in Sweden, the American publisher is Gareth Stevens, 1555 No. River Center Drive, Suite 201, Milwaukee, WI 53212.

Froschl, Merle; Colon, Linda; Rubin, Ellen and Sprung, Barbara. (1984). *Including All of Us: An Early Curriculum About Disability*. New York: Educational Equity Concepts, Inc.

Paasche, Gorrill, Strom. (1990). *Children With Special Needs in Early Childhood Settings*. Reading, MA: Addison-Wesley.

Excellent resource! For each of 33 disabilities gives a definition, physical and behavioral characteristics, recommendations on things to do and resources.

Wolery, Mark and Wilbers, Jan S. (1994). *Including Children With Special Needs in Early Childhood Programs*. Research monograph published by the National Association for the Education of Young Children, vol. 6.

Other information

An excellent summary of the parts of The Americans with Disabilities Act of 1992 that affect child care providers can be ordered by sending $6.00 to: NCCA, 1029 Railroad Street, Conyers, GA 30207.

If you wish to have the complete Act, order *The Americans with Disabilities Handbook,* published by the Equal Employment Opportunity Commission (EEOC) and the U.S. Department of Justice (DOJ). The part applicable to child care facilities is Title III, Nondiscrimination on the Basis of Disability by Public Accommodations and in Commercial Facilities. To order, call the EEOC at 800-669-EEOC or the DOJ at 202-514-0301.

National Information Center for Children and Youth with Disabilities (NICHCY) P.O. Box 1492, Washington, DC 20013-1492. This organization publishes a News Digest three times a year. Individual subscriptions are free. Also available from NICHCY is a Parent's Guide, to help families learn how to get help for their young children with special needs (birth through five years). For a NICHCY publications list send a letter to above address or call 1-800-999-5599.

To understand more about child care and the ADA:

Understanding the ADA: Information for Early Childhood Programs available free from:
> National Association for the Education of Young Children
> Box ADA
> 1509 16th Street NW
> Washington, DC 20036
> 800-422-2460

Caring for Children with Special Needs: The ADA and Child Care.,
Child Care and the ADA: Highlights for Parents, and *Child Care and the ADA: Highlights for Parents of Children with Disabilities* available from:
> The Child Care Law Center
> 22 Second Street, 5th Floor
> San Francisco, CA 94105
> 415-495-5498

The ADA and Child Care Providers available from:
> Action for Better Child Care
> United Cerebral Palsy of Greater Atlanta
> 1776 Peachtree Street NW, Suite 522S
> Atlanta, GA 30309
> 404-892-2252

Head Start materials

The Head Start Bulletin, which is published six times a year by the U.S. Department of Health and Human Services, contains much information of value to parents and teachers.

Contact: Head Start Bulletin, P.O. Box 1182, Washington, DC 20013.

(Note: Issue #45 includes a list of Disability Organizations which have information, publications or materials on disabilities.)

Organizations

American Council of the Blind
1010 Vermont Ave., NW Suite 1100
Washington, DC 20005
202-467-5081

Learning Disabilities Association of America
4156 Library Road
Pittsburg, PA 15234
412-341-1515

Association for the Education and Rehabilitation of the Blind and
Visually Impaired
206 N. Washington Street, Suite 320
Alexandria, VA 22314

Association for Retarded Citizens
259 Bailey #A
Fort Worth, TX 76107
817-877-1474

Council for Exceptional Children
1920 Association Drive
Reston, VA 22091
703-620-3660

Easter Seal Society
2023 West Ogden Avenue
Chicago, IL 60612
312-551-7100

March of Dimes Birth Defects Foundation
1275 Mamaroneck Rd.
White Plains, NY 10605
914-428-7100

United Cerebral Palsy Associations, Inc.
7 Penn Plaza, Suite 804
New York, NY 10001
212-677-7400

Mistakes
Adults
Make

PARENTS LOVE THEIR CHILDREN and want them to be happy, and teachers want to do the very best they can for the children in their care. So why do these well-meaning people make mistakes?

One reason is a lack of knowledge about the ages and stages of child development. This can result in two year olds being scolded for doing what is perfectly normal for that age or being pushed to achieve something that is well beyond them. A five year old, on the other hand, may be capable of doing more than parents and teachers realize and be frustrated by not being allowed to try new things.

Perhaps parents are doing what was done unto them. If they were treated with sarcasm, that is what the children will hear. If protests were always answered with "Because I said so," that will be their almost automatic response when they hear, "Why can't I?"

Sometimes adults simply do not seem to hear themselves or realize how much their remarks can hurt. These same adults would not dream of striking a child, but they may not be aware of the impact of careless words.

We hope that this section will help parents and teachers become more aware of their own actions and find ways to turn the negative into something positive.

Lucille & Zachary

"Loretta, this child doesn't know her colors!"

Lucille

"Come here and sit with me, Lucille," said Esther Richards in a voice that sounded more like a command than an invitation.

Her not quite three year old niece went obediently and climbed up on the sofa.

"Let's play a color game," said her aunt. "See if you can show me two red things." Lucille looked around, then reached out and touched an orange cushion and her own purple dress.

Esther Richards frowned. "Loretta, this child doesn't know her colors!" she exclaimed. "I remember that your Rachel knew her colors when she was only two. Is Lucille slow in other things? Does she know the alphabet? Rachel used to sing me the alphabet song when she was younger than this."

"Lucille is fine," said Loretta Kramer defensively. "She may not be quite as bright as Rachel, but Rachel has always been very advanced for her age. Lucille does as well as most of the other children in her child care center."

I guess I'll never be as good as Rachel, thought Lucille, while five year old Rachel was thinking complacently, I'm smarter than the other children. Mother said so.

Zachary

"What a handsome little boy," remarked Ellen Morales, nodding toward a sturdy, curly-haired four year old. Ellen had come to the Happy Days Child Care Center to take pictures of all the children.

"Yes, Zachary is a cute kid," agreed his teacher. "It's a good thing. He's going to have to get by on good looks, because he sure isn't going to make it on brains. He's developmentally delayed, and he's more than two years behind the other children. He likes to color, but his papers are just scribbles, not pictures."

"But doesn't 'delayed' mean that he'll catch up sooner or later?" asked Ellen.

"Oh, it's supposed to, but I think they call it that to make parents feel better. Personally, I don't think this kid will ever get very far."

The two adults moved away. Zachary looked down at the crayon in his hand, then threw it on the floor. He sat by himself for the rest of the day, shaking his head when his friends wanted him to play.

When Zachary told his mother he didn't want to go to school any more, she explained to him that she had a job, and that was the only school near enough for her to take him there. "It's really a very nice place," she assured him. To herself she thought, he probably had a squabble with one of the other children, but he'll get over it. At first she failed to notice that Zach no longer used the crayons he had always loved, and was unusually silent. It's hard for a working mother to do her job, get meals, do the laundry and all the other tasks involved in maintaining a family. However, she thought he would eventually use the crayons and learn to like school again.

Respect all children

NEVER discuss children in their presence. Adults sometimes act as if children were marble statues with no ears. Would two adults stand beside another adult and talk about him or her in a negative and hurtful way? There is no way of measuring how much damage was done to Zachary's already fragile self-confidence, or "I Am," but certainly his disability was compounded by the teacher's remarks. Fortunately, Zachary's teacher represents the exception, not the rule.

Never compare children, especially siblings. In the first story, Esther and Loretta were making another grave error, also a common one. They were comparing two sisters. Rarely do two siblings develop in the same way. It is unfair to make any child feel ashamed because he or she doesn't measure up to the pattern set by an older brother or sister. It isn't good for the older child, either, to get an over-inflated sense of self-importance.

Keep expectations high for all children. No teacher has a right to make negative assumptions about a child's ability, no matter what the "experts" have said. A number of studies and experiments have shown that a child will perform according to a teacher's expectations. If you expect children to learn well or behave well, they will. If you expect the opposite, that's usually what you will get.

We have all read many stories about doctors who have said, "He'll never walk!" "She'll never be more than two years old, mentally," only to be proved wrong by parents who would not give up.

Parents, teachers and professionals need to work together. When any child in a school has a problem that is enough out of the ordinary for someone to have tested, diagnosed and named the condition, the information should go to the parents, and from them to the director. It is then up to that director to work with the people who will be involved with the child. The teachers need to understand just what the condition is, the teaching approach to be used and the importance of their own expectations.

The majority of parents have not had the education in child development which might help them spot the warning signs of trouble. On the other hand, the school director, at the very least, should have a strong background in this area, and if the teachers in the school do not, it is up to the director to provide this education. Even without such training, teachers who see many children may be the first to notice when something is not quite right.

21

Out on a limb

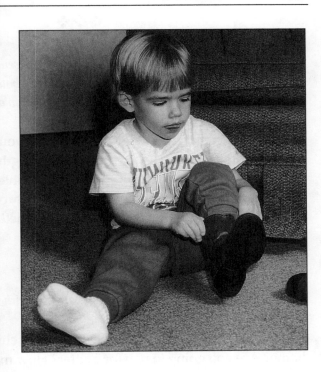

"Stop wasting your time and get your boots on, or the van will leave without you."

Anyone can make a mistake

It's a rare parent or teacher who does not, at some time, lose patience and snap out a threat that doesn't make sense. When the hasty words you have just spoken echo back in your mind, and you realize what you have done, back up! Do it promptly, and if possible, with a shrug and a rueful smile. You can teach a valuable lesson by showing a child that anyone can make a mistake, and there is a way to handle it.

"Did you hear what I just said? That didn't make sense! I guess I was so angry that I just didn't stop to think. We need to think about this together, and come up with an idea that will help you remember not to do that again."

Show children that it is all right to admit that you are wrong, and model for them how to handle it. This will strengthen your authority by dealing firmly and fairly with the initial problem. Let children know what is going to happen, consistently carry through, and they will not be left feeling that they "got away with" something.

"If you don't clean up your room, you can't go with us to the circus."

Really? Are you going to take the other three children and leave Anita home? Are you going to pay for a sitter? How much will you enjoy the circus, thinking of Anita crying in her room?

"Anita, I'm sorry I said that. I really don't want you to miss the circus, so I will help you clean your room this time, but from now on I want you to put your toys away after you use them."

"How dare you talk back to me! You march yourself right down to the office and tell the principal what you just said to me!"

How do you think the principal is going to feel about that? He may keep Billy in the office, cooling his heels and getting anxious, before talking with him. But what is he going to think of you as a teacher? And is all of that going to change Billy's attitude so he will respect you, so he won't back talk again?

"Billy, I take that back. This is our problem, not Mr. Turrisi's. I need to know what has made you so angry with me, and you need to know that I cannot accept back talk from any of my students."

"Stop wasting time and get your boots on, or the van will go without you."

And if the school van does go without Lester, who is going to take this four year old child home? That's right. You are!

"It's all right, Lester, you are going to be on the van. I'll help you, and tomorrow I'll make sure you start ten minutes earlier so you will have time to do it yourself."

"Margo, if you had been paying attention in math class, you would have been able to finish that math paper. Now you can just stay and do it after school!"

Uh oh! You forgot that you have company coming for dinner tonight, and you wanted to go straight home and get everything ready.

"I really wasn't thinking when I said that, Margo. Let me look at your paper. If you don't understand how to do it, I'll arrange time to help you."

"Ellie, you spoiled the story for everyone by acting silly. You'll have to stay in the director's office while the rest of us go outside to play."

You're going to be in more trouble than Ellie on this one. You know what Ms. Jarvis will say about your taking a four year old child's outdoor play time away.

"I spoke too fast, Ellie. I want you to have your play time, but we need to set up some rules for everyone about story time. If you don't want to listen to a story, you may play quietly in the doll corner, with a puzzle or with crayons and paper. You may not play with anything noisy or interrupt the story, because that isn't fair to the children who do want to listen."

22

Don't make them lie

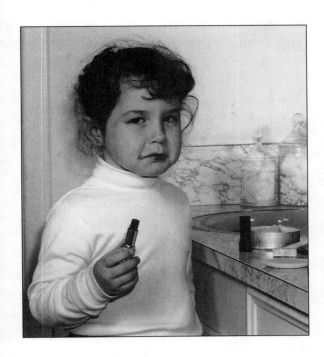

"Did you pinch the baby again?"

Steve

Pam Butler was in the kitchen preparing lunch when she heard four month old Ashley screaming. As she hurried into the baby's room, Pam saw bright red pinch marks on Ashley's arm, fading into white. "Steve," she cried angrily, "did you pinch the baby again?"

Amanda

Pete Houlihan was tired when he came home from work. It had been a hot day, and he was glad to change out of his business suit into cooler sport clothes. On his mind, however, was the report he needed to put on the computer for the next morning's meeting. When his wife told him supper wouldn't be ready for about an hour, he decided to get the job done then so he could relax later.

The minute he walked into the study, he knew something was wrong. His computer screen was on, and a jumble of characters filled the brightly lit screen.

He went back to the kitchen. "Marge," he asked, "has Amanda been near my computer today?"

"Yes, she came out of the study a little while ago, just as I came downstairs," answered his wife. "Is something wrong?"

"You could say so," answered her husband in a grim tone, and he went to the foot of the stairs. "Amanda, come down here!" he shouted.

His six year old daughter came slowly down the stairs. "Amanda," said Steve in ominous tones, "were you fooling around with my computer? Answer me!"

Jenny

Shana Randall stopped short in dismay as she walked into her bedroom. The top of her dressing table was a mess. Lipsticks opened, a white film of powder over everything and a smear of bright red nail polish had soaked into the lacy bureau runner, making it stick to the white wood underneath.

Shana hurried downstairs, went into the living room and snapped off the television program her four year old daughter was watching.

"Jenny," she demanded accusingly, "were you playing with my make-up? Did you spill that nail polish all over my dressing table?"

Lie and be punished or tell the truth and be punished

Steve, Amanda and Jenny knew at once that they were in trouble. They were facing angry grown-ups. Admitting guilt meant punishment, even four year old Jenny knew that. Saying "No" meant punishment, too, for lying. But most children will say "No" when caught in a situation like this. Maybe they will embellish the denial with a story to explain what happened. "A bee stung the baby." "The cat walked on the computer keys." "The wind blew over the nail polish."

Teach, don't punish!

In each of these cases, the parents knew the child was guilty. If they pushed the child into an admission of guilt or a lie, the next step was punishment.

The real problem was that Steve didn't want that baby, that interloper, around. Mom never seemed to have time to do things with him any more. A spanking might hurt, and it might deter him for a while, but until the issue of sibling rivalry was addressed, he would pinch the baby again.

Amanda was fascinated by her father's computer. She had seen how he turned it on, and the magical way words came up on the screen. It was a shock to find that it didn't work that well for her, but sooner or later, she knew she would figure it out. If she was punished by not being allowed to play at her best friend's house for a week, it would make her sad, but would not keep her from watching for a chance to try that computer again.

Jenny loved watching her pretty mother put on her make-up. She wanted to try all those magical bottles and jars and tubes. She never meant to spill that nail polish—it just slipped out of her hand when she tried to unscrew the top. Not being allowed to watch "Sesame Street" for a week might keep her away from the make-up, but would she realize that she should not play with the clothes and shoes in her mother's closet or the jewelry in the gold box?

Explain why you are upset

Involve older children in caring for younger siblings. Help children understand why the action was wrong. Steve's mother could talk to him about the helplessness of a small baby, and how important it is for a big brother to protect a baby from pain, not inflict it. Involving Steve in the care of the baby, and setting aside time to spend alone with Steve will also help him adjust to a new baby sister. She should *not* pinch Steve to show how it hurt. Instead, she could remind Steve of the pain he felt when he fell off a swing or was stung by a bee.

Spend time with children doing things they are interested in. Amanda's dad could show his daughter the report he had to prepare, explain how important it was, and how important it was to have the computer in perfect working order. He could talk about how expensive a computer was. In addition, he could promise to teach Amanda how to use it, starting the next Saturday, but only if she promised *never* to touch it without permission.

Involve children in cleaning up messes they created. Jenny's mother could have Jenny help her clean up the spilled powder, show her the ruined lace runner and have Jenny help her remove the polish from the white wood.

Lois's Story

Are we saying you should not punish a child for doing something he or she knew was wrong? No, but perhaps the following true story will suggest a way to handle situations like this.

When I was in second grade, I used to walk to school each day with several friends. On the way we passed a little corner store that had a wonderful selection of penny candy. In those days, a penny might buy three tootsie rolls, two licorice sticks or eight jelly beans.

Every day, one of my friends would have two or three pennies, or maybe even a nickel. We would all offer eager advice, but the one with the money made the decision and passed around the candy.

I don't remember that I was ever left out. There was always a piece of candy for me, but it bothered me more and more that I was never the buyer, never the one to show my generosity. But in my house, an allowance was unheard of, and pennies were never passed out.

I took a quarter. *Then one morning, I went through the kitchen on my way out the door. My mother's little black change purse was on the kitchen table, and it was open. Not only was it open, it was full of change. What little demon whispered in my ear, "She'll never miss one quarter?" The next minute I was gone, the quarter clutched in my hand.*

That day my friends and I were almost late for school, it took so long to decide how to spend that quarter. There was enough for all those who had so often treated me, and still some left to be passed around at recess. I felt like a kindly queen, passing out largesse to her adoring subjects. It was wonderful—until I was on my way home. The candy was gone, and I came down to earth with a thud. Why had I ever thought my mother wouldn't miss a huge amount like a quarter? Why hadn't I taken a nickel? She might not have noticed that. Why had I taken anything at all? What was going to happen to me?

The minute I went in the door, my worst fears were confirmed. My mother stood there, looking at me sorrowfully. "Lois, go up to your room," she said in a sober voice. "Your father will be up in a little while."

I ran up to my bedroom and flung myself on the bed, sobbing. My father had never even spanked me, but that was because I hadn't ever done anything really bad. Now I was sure that I was in for a spanking, or even worse. (A child who reads a lot develops a fertile imagination!) It seemed like forever before I heard Papa's steps on the stairs. He sat down on the bed and looked at me, but when he spoke, his voice wasn't angry, it was sad.

Trust is based on truth. "Lois, you did a very bad thing this morning. You stole some money from your mother's purse. I won't ask you if you did it, because if you should lie to me, that would just make things worse. What you have done was to break trust. Trust is a very important word. It means that we can always know that you will do what is right. We don't have to worry about leaving a change purse on the table, because we know you won't touch it. We know that if we ask you a question, you will always tell us the truth. If people don't trust you, they will never believe you, will never feel they can count on you. It would make your mother and me very sad to think we could never trust you again."

"Oh, Papa, I'm sorry!" I cried, tears pouring down my face. "I'll never take anything again. I promise!"

"I believe you," he said gently. "You made a mistake, but now you know better, and I believe that from now on we can trust you. Now go wash your face and come help your mother get supper ready."

That was one of the most important lessons of my life. A spanking I would have forgotten, but those words stayed with me all my life and have kept me from yielding to even minor temptations. It was a lesson that I passed on to my children, and now I offer it to you.

Caught in the "Because I said so!" trap

"Eddie, come back here. You cannot climb that tower."

Mrs. Dee's tone was exasperated. The carefully planned field trip to a local park was being spoiled by this one obstreperous first-grader. It seemed to her that she had done nothing the whole time but say "No!" to Eddie. Now he was glaring at her defiantly from the bottom rung of the forty foot tower before them.

"Why?" *he challenged.* "I climbed it when I was here with my dad."

The teacher's mind went back to the year before. One boy had climbed almost to the top then froze, and she had to go up after him. It wasn't an experience she wanted to repeat.

"No!" she repeated.

"Why?" he answered.

Just then Katie, another child in the class, spoke up. "Because Mrs. Dee's the teacher and she said so!" she said firmly. Eddie hesitated a moment, then reluctantly stepped to the ground and came towards them.

"The truth of the matter is," Louise Dee admitted when she told this story to her husband, "I didn't want to say that to him—'Because I said so.' I remember how frustrated it made me when I was a little girl and that was the answer my father gave to everything. He never listened to my side. I promised myself I would never say that to a child, that I would always explain when I had to say 'No.' The trouble is, children don't always accept a reasonable explanation. They just come back with another 'why' and you find yourself arguing forever."

It's a lucky parent or teacher who has never been caught in this trap. Not all children push adults this way, but when it happens, it's a power struggle. The adult's patience runs out, and out come those words: "Because I said so!"

Caught in the trap

The adult's patience is gone. Connie Rocha, the person mentioned in Chapter 9, hates to let a child push her into that overused and weak response. She developed her own approach. With her permission, we'll share with you a story she told us.

She was cooking spinach for the noon meal when Pedro came to the kitchen door, sniffing.

"Are you cookin' spinach?" he asked suspiciously.

"Yes, I am," she replied.

"Why are you doin' that?" he demanded. "You know we don't like spinach."

"I don't like it either, but I have to cook it," was her answer.

"Why?"

Connie turned off the heat and led him to her office. "Come in here and I'll show you. Do you see that paper on the wall?" She pointed to her license, with its gold seal. He nodded.

"That's the paper the mayor gave me that says I can have this school."

Then she took down a copy of the licensing regulations, a large, unwieldy book. She sat down and began turning the pages, murmuring aloud as she did. "Ah, here it is, spinach. Let's see what it says."

Rely on an impartial authority. Pedro looked at her wide-eyed as she ran her finger along the line and "read" aloud, "Ms. Rocha must cook spinach one day a week or I will take away her paper." She shrugged. "You see? That's just the way it is."

Pedro nodded solemnly and went back to the other children. From the kitchen she heard him saying, "Look, you kids, we gotta eat that spinach or Ms. Rocha can't have this school any more."

The next time you find yourself backed into a no-win confrontation, take a leaf out of Connie's book. Let an outsider settle the matter, one whose authority is indisputable, and better yet, one who is not there to have to answer those endless "Why's?"

24

"And the winner is..."

Making
children
compete
with each
other

"Hey, Evelyn, I've got a great idea!" Ed Gleason's ruddy face was beaming with enthusiasm. "The last week of summer school, I think we ought to have a Field Day. I'll set up the events and get the kids ready. If there isn't enough money in the budget to buy prizewinners' ribbons, I'll make some. We can invite the parents. The kids will love it."

This is what I was afraid of, thought Evelyn Gardner. How do I handle this without hurting Ed's feelings? It's hard enough for him to be working under a woman, and one so much younger than he is. He means well, but I can't let him do something that goes against the whole purpose of this program.

Evelyn was working for a public school system in the suburbs of a large northern city. The school committee had authorized a six week summer enrichment program for children from kindergarten through sixth grade. Because Evelyn had been directing a very successful individualized program in one of the larger schools, she had been offered the job of planning and directing this program.

Although the parents had to pay a modest tuition, 240 children were enrolled. Many of them were there because their parents worked and needed a place where their children would be safe and happy during the long days of summer vacation. Others had been eager to sign up because they had heard about what was going on during the school year. The WAG program (We Are Great) was built on the idea that all children should be allowed to learn as individuals, at a speed which would allow them to succeed. The program boosted the children's self-esteem and showed them that learning was fun and exciting.

Ed Gleason was a retired Physical Education teacher who had only worked with high school boys. She had wondered how he would fit into this program, but the Superintendent of Schools had made the hiring decision for her.

She smiled. "Tell me more about it, Ed," she invited. "For example, what kinds of events, and what do you mean when you say 'get the kids ready?'"

"Well, the kinds of events you have in a gym program," he said. "Running races, of course, and broad jumping and high jumping, and maybe hurdles for the older children. If we used the gym, we could have some rope climbing. We have four weeks for them to practice, and to see who qualifies for the different events. We'd have gold ribbons for first prize, blue for second, red for third."

Set up situations so every child can succeed

"You said the kids would love it," said Evelyn. "What about the ones who don't win any ribbons? With the set-up you describe, we would have winners, but we would also have losers. Yes, a Field Day would be fun, but only if every child can win a ribbon."

Ed's face turned red. "That's crazy," he protested. "You need competition. That's what makes kids push themselves to excel. Naturally, they can't all win. It takes the meaning out of winning."

"You may be right," said Evelyn. "But in WAG our goal isn't for children to push themselves to be better than someone else. However..."

"You probably think we shouldn't have a gym program at all," he interrupted angrily.

There's a way to make every child a winner. "I'm very much in favor of physical activity," said Evelyn. "I'll admit, I thought each teacher could take care of that. When the superintendent said he felt we should have a gym program, I was reluctant. But I have already seen that you have an expertise that most of our teachers don't have. You have been trained to know which exercises are good for growing children, and you can teach the older children a lot about team sports like softball. I've noticed that you stress good sportsmanship, and that's great. Just the same, I think there's a way to make every child a winner. It's a matter of doing some creative thinking."

He frowned. "What does that mean?" he demanded truculently.

Each child competes with himself or herself. "Encourage each child to compete with himself or herself. Let the children choose which activities they want to participate in, and keep records of what they can do now. How fast *they run, how far or how high they jump, etc. I have to tell you, I just happened to see Randy yesterday when he topped his own record in the high jump. If I had been able to get a picture of the glow on his face, this conversation wouldn't have to take place. When I praised him, his answer was, 'Gee, thanks—but I can do better than that.'*

Reward all the children's accomplishments. *"On Field Day, you have prizes for Susy, who ran the 100 yard dash faster than she did at the beginning, for Freddie, who learned to hop and hopped ten feet, for Chan, who jumped a foot farther, etc. You can have a prize for Tammy, who tried so hard, for Jimmy, who always had a smile... I'm sure you'll think of others. You can still have a fastest runner, a highest jumper, etc., but they will all receive gold ribbons, and they will all be winners."*

"I see what you mean," he said thoughtfully. "I don't think that the high school kids I used to teach would have gone for it, but I guess in a special program like this it might work. Okay, if that's what you want, I'll try it."

When this true episode took place, in the mid-seventies, the importance of making every child a winner, or, conversely, no child a loser, was not as widely understood as it is today. What happens to the self-esteem of the chubby second grader who hasn't yet lost his baby fat, the awkward child who hasn't learned how to manage her body, the child who is never chosen to be "on a team" in any game or sport?

Choose activities and games that allow everyone to take part. With preschool children especially, there is no room for competition. A parent or teacher should always think, "Does this set one child against another, or can they *all* take part and have fun together?" Every child should be able to get into the act—to participate at her own level and have FUN—to know the special joy of shouting, "I DID IT!"

"How many times have I told you...?"

Nagging, scolding and repeating

Claire Foster closed the door on the last child to leave the child care center and leaned against it wearily. "I am absolutely beat," she said to the other teacher who was already busy putting toys away and straightening up the room.

"It's a hard job," agreed the other sympathetically. "You've only been here a month; you're still adjusting."

"I never realized how much bending and stretching and lifting there would be," said Claire, "but what really gets to me is that I never seem to get anywhere with the children. I try to teach them how to do things, but they never listen. Do you have that trouble, Janice?"

"Not really," said her friend. "Perhaps you are trying too hard. Try to relax and enjoy them. They are really sweet kids, you know. Come on, this place looks pretty good. Time to leave. Go home, put your feet up and have a cup of tea. That was my mother's answer to everything."

That may be good advice, mused Claire as she drove home, but it won't make those kids learn to pay attention. Maybe I'll go talk to the director tomorrow and see if she can tell me what to do.

Children "tune out" nagging

If Claire had been running a tape recorder in her room all day, what would she have heard when she played the tape?

- ♦ "Edward, don't touch that truck. That's Guido's truck, he brought it to school."

- ♦ "Mandy, look at your hands. There's paint on them, so I know you didn't wash before coming to snack. How many times have I told you children to wash your hands before snack?"

- ♦ "Edward, I just told you to stay away from Guido's truck!"

- ♦ "Look at these jars of paint—they are all ruined—I'll have to throw them away. The paint looks like mud. How many times have I told you all to wash the brush before you start to use another color?"

♦ "Owen, watch out! You've spilled your milk again. How many times do I have to tell you not to put your cup so near the edge of the table! You never listen."

♦ "Nora, you're not going to be ready for the school bus. Everyone, help Nora find her other boot. I've told you all a thousand times to put your boots in the bottom of your cubby when you take them off."

Claire was right about one thing—the children were not listening. When a teacher nags and scolds and repeats directions over and over, children quickly learn to "tune out." What would Claire's director say to her?

Teach children, don't just tell them what to do

Telling children isn't *teaching* them. Give more thought to your approach.

Model behavior for the children to follow. Instead of standing on one side of the room and calling across to Edward, go over to him, sit down with him, and tell him what he *can* do, not what he mustn't do. "Edward, when you play with the toys in the school, you don't have to ask. But when someone brings a favorite toy in from home, try asking politely, 'Guido, may I please hold your truck for a little bit?' If he says no, then you'll have to go play with something else, but he may very well say yes."

Build good habits into the daily routine. What about Mandy's hands, and all the children's hands? It is very important for *all* of the children to learn how to wash their hands thoroughly and to get in the habit of doing it. Have a group lesson. Go through the motions first, showing how you rub the fronts and backs of your hands and wrists. Then show them with soap. Work up a good lather, make "soap gloves." Rinse thoroughly and dry them with a paper towel. Ask for volunteers, and while two at a time go through the routine, the others can watch to see if they forgot anything.

Then talk about germs, how they get on everything they play with, and how those germs will get on their food if they don't get rid of the pesky creatures with soap and water. This tells them why it is especially important to wash before eating.

Begin slowly and build on successful experiences. In the first stages of painting, children aren't ready to use several colors. Begin with one color (let them choose the one they want). Show them how to clean the brush in water when they are all through painting, so it will be ready for the next painter.

To show them what happens when they don't clean the brush, put four or five colors in bottle caps and mix them by dipping the brush in first one then another, till all the paint looks muddy.

When they have mastered using one color and rinsing out the brush, let them try two colors. Add additional colors one at a time, as they seem ready. Allow plenty of time— weeks, maybe months. They may not get beyond two colors at all during the year that you have them.

Organize the classroom and the home. To avoid milk spills, make place mats with a circle for the plate and a smaller one in the upper right hand corner for the cup. You might even make these in washable plastic and glue an inexpensive coaster where the cup goes, one with a slight rim.

What about boots? One of the best gimmicks I have seen for boots is the spring type clothespin with the child's name on it. Have all the children practice clipping their boots together. If they use hooks on the wall instead of cubbies, help them learn to read their names and put the boots right under their coats.

Are you thinking you won't have time for your daily program if you have to spend so much time on things like this? This *is* program. Besides, think of the time you'll save when you don't have to repeat yourself over and over!

26

"Tell him you're sorry!"

Making young children apologize

"You pushed Kimo and made him bump his head. It hurts, and he is crying. Tell him you're sorry!" Ms. Lockwood's voice wasn't just stern, it was angry.

"No!" Four year old Mateo answered defiantly. "He pushed me first. He's always pushing. I hate him. I'm not sorry."

The teacher took Mateo by the hand and marched him over to a chair set apart in one corner of the room. "You sit right here until you are ready to apologize to Kimo."

Jean Lockwood turned to the other children, who were looking at her with a mixture of dismay and curiosity. They are waiting to see what I will do if Mateo doesn't apologize, she thought, and I don't know what I'll do. Do I make him miss snack? Send him to another room while my class has recess? How did I get into this, anyway?

Help children understand why an apology is important

Insisting that children apologize for their misbehavior, whether it was deliberate or accidental, rarely solves any problems, and as Jean Lockwood was finding out, it can make matters worse. None of the thoughts running through her mind were appropriate. Snack and outdoor play time are an important part of each child's program, and withholding them must never be used as punishment.

To a two year old, the words, "I'm sorry," have no real meaning. Let's think about the words, "I'm sorry," and what they mean to different children. To a two year old, the words have no real meaning. They may repeat the phrase after you, as they repeat any new words you teach them, but they rarely understand what they are saying, and will probably repeat the offense five minutes later.

However, at that age you can make a beginning. "What you said to Olivia made her sad. See, she's crying. When we make someone cry, we say 'I'm sorry' to the person." That's enough. Don't belabor it. You are laying the foundation for the day when they can make the connection between wrongdoing and repentance.

A three year old can follow up an apology with help. Three year old Jed will say the words of apology after bumping into Caitlin and causing her to knock the doll dishes off the table in the dramatic play area, but they are just words. He doesn't follow through with action. This is when you can say, "Oh my, Caitlin's dishes are on the floor. You said you were sorry, and that is good, but it would be even better if you helped her pick up the dishes and put them back on the table." This kind of approach may well end up with Jed sharing a tea party with Caitlin.

As children get older and understand what the words "apologize" and "I'm sorry" mean, they may also be reaching the stage where they are taking words very literally, as in the story about Mateo and Kimo.

How can I teach children to apologize?

Jean Lockwood's words led directly to a confrontation. What might she have said?

Your own words and actions are the best way to teach children. "When people start pushing each other, someone usually gets hurt. It makes me sad when this happens. Kimo, I'm sorry you got hurt, and Mateo, I'm sorry Kimo made you so angry you felt you had to push him."

The teacher has acknowledged that both children were at fault, and she has apologized *for* them. Both children will feel better. They may or may not say those difficult words this time, but they are more apt to do so the next time.

Help children understand that an apology is a promise to stop hurting another person. Some children use the words "I'm sorry" as a way of doing whatever they want to and getting away with it. When this happens, usually at about five and up, the teacher needs to deal with it. "Felicia, you said you were sorry you called George names and hurt his feelings, but I don't think you meant your apology because you kept right on using those mean words. You cannot do something you know is wrong and think you can make up for it by apologizing. You show that you are really growing up when you think about what you are saying and stop before you hurt someone."

Instead of demanding apologies, what can we do? Your own words and actions are the best way to teach children both the words "I'm sorry" and the meaning behind them.

Finally, a note of encouragement. Most children will instinctively try to comfort a child who has been hurt. Erik may have thrown a stone that hit Megan, but when he sees her crying, he is quite likely to run over and put his arms around her, saying "Don't cry, Megan." Children have a lot of love to give!

27

"Let Terry play with your truck."

Making young children share

"Terry is your guest. You share your things with a guest. Let Terry play with your truck." Stewart Madore's voice was stern, his look cold and disapproving.

Three year old Rodney wrapped both arms around his red fire truck and held it tightly. "No!" he shouted defiantly. "It's my special truck. Grandma gave it to me for my birthday. I don't want Terry to play with it."

His father's look became even sterner. "Rodney, I am ashamed of you. You are being selfish. Go to your room, and leave the truck here. I'll take Terry home now. I'm sure he'd rather play with someone who knows how to share."

Rodney burst into tears, dropped the truck and ran from the room. "I hate you!" he screamed between sobs.

When Stewart Madore returned from driving Terry home, his wife was waiting for him. "I heard all that from the kitchen," she said. "I didn't come in because we agreed not to interfere with each other in matters of discipline, but I think you were wrong. He's only three years old, Stewart, and now he's upstairs crying his eyes out. How could you be so mean to him?"

Her husband looked uncomfortable. "Tracy, he has to learn. He was not only selfish, he defied me. I can't let him get away with that. You have to show children you mean what you say or they won't respect you."

When is it reasonable to expect children to share?

Tracy was right to talk with her husband, but neither of them understood why something that should have been a minor incident blew up into a major problem.

Stewart used three words that did not have real meaning to Rodney—sharing, guest and selfish.

A young child has difficulty sharing. A child who has just recently turned three hasn't had time to learn the concept of sharing. He knows *mine,* and he felt quite justified in keeping what was his. It takes time for any person to discover the pleasure that comes from making someone else happy by sharing something special.

The idea of a guest having special rights was new to Rodney. Terry was his friend, someone he played with. The fact that Terry had come to play at his house did not seem to Rodney to be any reason to have to give up his favorite toy. If that was being *selfish*, Rodney didn't care.

Children learn these concepts from a number of experiences, from conversations in words they can understand, and above all, from example.

Does Rodney see his father offer his favorite chair to a guest? On the other hand, has he ever heard his mother say, "I guess I'll put away that good box of chocolates I got for my birthday before my friends come to play bridge, or they'll be all gone in one day."

How can you help children learn to share?

Let him know he will get the toy back shortly. Instead of "Let Terry play with your truck," Stewart could have said, "You have been playing with your truck. It would be nice if you let Terry have a turn, and pretty soon it will be your turn again, and he will give it back. However, it is your truck, and if you really don't want him to use it, we will put it away until you are playing alone."

Give words to the feeling you are trying to foster. "You really made Terry happy when you let him have a turn with your truck."

Recognize and reward what he has done. "I am glad that you shared your truck with Terry. You are learning to be a good friend."

Help children understand what you want them to do, and let them feel the warmth of your approval. You will both feel much better about the results.

28

"I can do it myself!"

The
unintentional
put-down

Peter
"I'm not very good
at cutting."

*Four year old Peter frowned with concentration. Carefully, he manipulated
the small scissors to cut around the circle on the paper he was holding. He was
cutting a little bit off the line, but not very much. Peter was feeling very pleased*

---

with his efforts when Mrs. Rich reached over his shoulder and plucked the scissors and paper out of his hand.

"I'll do that for you, Peter," said his teacher briskly.

"I can do it!" he said, reaching for the paper.

"No, dear, you aren't really big enough yet to cut on a line. See how crooked this is? I'll make you a new one."

Peter's shoulders sagged. I guess I'm not really very good at cutting, he thought. I'm not very good at anything. I'd better let her do the rest of my clock. I can't do it right.

Meredith
"She thinks I can't decide anything for myself."

"Meredith, why are you wearing jeans? I put out your plaid dress for you to wear today." Mrs. Nutley's tone was frazzled.

"But Mother," protested eight year old Meredith. "All the girls wear jeans to school. We play softball at recess, and I can run faster in jeans. I might fall down, and the dress could get torn."

"Then maybe you shouldn't play softball. You look so pretty in your nice little dresses. I want to be proud of my little girl."

Meredith's lower lip stuck out mutinously as she went back to change. I can pick out my own clothes, she was thinking. I know when to wear a dress and when to wear jeans. She thinks I can't decide anything for myself.

Aaron
"Don't you trust me?"

"I'm really too busy to mow the lawn," said Ben Edelman. He turned to his twelve year old son. *"Aaron, I'll have to ask you to do it."*

"Sure, Dad," said Aaron eagerly. *This was the first time his father had trusted him to use the power mower. He felt very big and important.*

"I'll start it for you, and show you the best way to cut the grass," went on his father. *"If you don't do it right, you'll leave ridges of grass. And remember, this is not a toy. A power mower can be very dangerous if you don't handle it correctly."*

*"I **know** how to start it, and I'll be careful,"* Aaron cut in, *his face flushed with anger. "I said I'd do it. Let me do it myself! Don't you trust me?"*

Let children learn
from their mistakes

Parents and teachers strive to promote children's self-esteem. They want to encourage children to develop a strong *I Am! I Can!* But they chip away at a child's *I Am* whenever they offer help before it is needed. Young children should be given the chance to do things for themselves. What if the finished paper isn't perfect? The *I Can* will grow when they learn from their mistakes. Failure doesn't necessarily make a child feel stupid. It is a signal to try again and again—to finally experience the thrill of *I did it!* If four year old Jason cannot make the scissors work, he will ask for help, and that is when you give it—but wait until he asks.

Believe in their abilities so they will trust themselves. Parents who have had the tendency to take over, to make it easier, to protect their child against making a mistake, to get the job done faster, are really hanging on to control. The message they deliver is "I don't trust you, I don't believe in you, you aren't ready to think for yourself." Let children learn from their mistakes and they will develop into self-assured, competent adults who have experienced the wonderful excitement of *I did it!*

29

Quiet!

Shouting across a room

A few years ago, we conducted a cross-country survey of child care. We visited 120 child care facilities in 22 states, searching for the factors that made for quality.

One day we found ourselves in a very attractive school in a southern state. The building was new and well-equipped. The director welcomed us graciously. We saw a lot of interesting learning taking place, and the children seemed generally happy. The only thing that made us hesitate to call this a GREAT school was the noise level.

We don't expect preschool children to be silent; indeed, we would be suspicious if they were. But there is a difference between the voices and laughter of children who are working happily side-by-side and NOISE—the kind that sends you home every night with a headache. As children's voices go up, they become shrill, and the whole atmosphere changes. You get a feeling of irritability and frustration.

We looked around to see what was causing this kind of noise in a school that otherwise we had been admiring. It wasn't in every room, we realized. Then we saw it.

The noise got louder and louder. *A group of three year olds had come in from the playground, and the teacher wanted them to gather on the floor in front of her for singing. "Q-U-I-E-T," she shouted, clapping her hands. "EVERYONE SIT DOWN HERE IN FRONT OF ME. STOP TALKING AND LISTEN. LISTEN TO ME. IF YOU DON'T STOP TALKING, YOU CAN'T HEAR ME." Her strident voice rang out across the room. Did the children stop talking and sit down? No, they just talked louder to drown her out.*

In *I AM! I CAN! Keys to Quality Child Care,* Dr. Mitchell tells of the day a supervisor visited a fairly new child care center. The director was complaining to her that the acoustics in the building were terrible. It was, indeed, very noisy, but what stood out was the teacher's voice, "shouting, directing, filling the room with her importance."

Make no mistake—when your voice goes up, the children will always outshout you. The louder your voice is, the noisier the children will get. It never fails.

How can I quiet down a loud group?

Speak softly to two or three children. Sit down with two or three children and speak very softly, just to them. Say something that will make them smile or nod their heads eagerly. The children just out of hearing will move in and stop talking so they can hear what you are saying, and the circle will grow. When it is quiet, you go on to explain, in a normal speaking voice, what is going to happen next.

Move to the disturbance. If you see a disturbance twenty feet away, do not shout, "Hank, stop that pushing." Instead, move quickly to Hank's side, touch him on the shoulder to get his attention, lean down to eye level and say very quietly, "Please don't push, Hank. Tell me very softly what started this." When it comes to crossing space, let your feet do the traveling, not your voice!

An ounce of prevention

Having unreasonable expectations

Adults sometimes make the mistake of expecting their children to behave like grown-ups. They forget that children need time to learn the rules of society—how to behave in social situations, how to interpret new terminology, the ways of hospitality. The following two incidents described below show what can happen when parents take too much for granted.

Ingrid
"They're spoiling my dinner."

Ingrid Berglund was seething with resentment. Here they were, she and Eric, dressed in their best, sitting in a lovely restaurant, with a great meal in front of them, and she couldn't enjoy it. She thought of how long they had planned for a special evening to celebrate their thirtieth anniversary, of how carefully they had saved from their limited income so they could splurge on this occasion. She should be enjoying the piano music in the background, admiring the attractive way the food was presented, soaking in the atmosphere of candlelight and flowers, but instead, the evening was being utterly ruined by those obnoxious kids two tables away.

The children's voices dominated the room. The little boy, who looked about five years old, started by whining about everything that was set in front of him. He didn't like the grapefruit in his fruit cocktail. He wanted a hot dog, not chicken or roast beef, and he wanted to sit on the other side of the table. His sister looked about two years older, but her manners were no better. Her main reaction to everything the waiter brought was a loud, "Yuck!" She called her brother names, teased him when he spilled some food on the tablecloth and demanded to know why they had to come to "this dumb place." Neither child seemed to pay any attention to the parents, who began to yell at them, showing their frustration and embarrassment.

For goodness' sake, why didn't they take their children someplace where they could have their hot dogs and hamburgers? thought Ingrid angrily. Why did they have to bring them here and spoil my evening?

Ken and Lydia "I thought we had good kids, but tonight I wanted to disown them."

"Excuse me," said Ken Hunter politely to his mother and aunt. "I'll just go help Lydia put the food on the table."

"Where the heck is Sammy?" he muttered to his wife as the door to the dining room closed behind him. "Didn't he know Mother and Winifred were coming today?"

"Of course he knew," snapped Lydia. "We'll just have to go ahead without him. Put that meat loaf on the table while I dish up the vegetables."

Just then the back door slammed, and their nine year old son came in cheerfully, talking as he came through the door. "Guess what, we won the game." He stopped short, looking puzzled. "How come the table isn't set? Aren't we eating out here tonight?"

"I **told** you your grandmother and Aunt Winifred were coming to dinner tonight," said his mother angrily. His father looked at him grimly. "You're a mess, but there's no time to change. Dinner is ready now! Go wash your hands and face and come to the table—the dining room table."

As Ken and Lydia went into the other room carrying hot dishes, the two guests came through the archway from the living room. "The table looks lovely," said the elder Mrs. Hunter politely. "And everything smells delicious," added Winifred.

Lydia saw with dismay that eight year old Rita was still on the sofa, absorbed in her book. She had left it just long enough to say "Hello," and had been reading ever since, ignoring the talk going on around her. "Rita, dinner is on the table," she called sharply, and her daughter reluctantly put down the book and came.

All through dinner, Lydia was stiff with embarrassment. Rita was in another world, saying almost nothing. Sammy, on the other hand, cheerfully unaware of his uncombed hair and his rumpled clothes, monopolized the conversation with talk about the game that afternoon.

As soon as the meal was over, both children muttered "'Scuse me," and without waiting for permission, took their plates to the kitchen and rushed into the living room. In a minute they could be heard arguing about which television program they wanted to watch.

Ken pushed back his chair abruptly and stalked into the other room. "Neither of you is watching television tonight," he said. "Come back and clear the table, then come into the living room. Your grandmother and Aunt Winifred did not come here to watch television or listen to you argue about it."

No one really enjoyed the next hour. The children's resentment showed in their body language—their expressionless faces and stiff movements. All four grown-ups tried to make cheerful talk, but it really didn't work. It was a relief to everyone when the company said polite goodbyes and left.

Once the door had shut and the car was heard leaving, Ken turned to the children. "Go to your rooms, both of you," he ordered. "Right now I'm too angry to talk about it, but you can be sure we're going to discuss this tomorrow!" Both Rita and Sammy knew from the tone of their father's voice and the look on his face that this was no time to argue, and went silently up the stairs.

Ken turned to his wife and exploded. "What happened here tonight?" he demanded furiously. "I thought we had good kids, but tonight I wanted to disown them."

Lydia was struggling not to cry. "How do you think I feel? That was your mother and your aunt. It's the first time they have been to visit us since the children were very small. We thought it was great that they were moving near enough to come see us often, but they'll never want to come back, and they must both think I'm an awful mother."

"We're too upset to think about it tonight," said Ken. "Let's leave the dishes and the talk until tomorrow."

Prepare children for a new experience

What do these stories have in common? In each case, the parents had failed to *communicate* with their children, to prepare them for a new experience. What if the first parents had taken a different approach? Suppose they had sat down and said something like this:

"On Thursday night, we are going to a very nice restaurant for dinner. This is the kind of place where grown-ups go when they want to have an extra special time. When you first sit down, a waiter or waitress brings you a menu, and you decide what you want to eat. You don't ask for something that isn't on the menu, like a hot dog, and when your food comes, you say 'Thank you.' Sometimes there's music for you to listen to, and you can look around at the candles and vases of flowers and pictures on the walls. You will notice that people talk in quiet voices, so others can enjoy themselves. We've never taken you anyplace like this before, but we believe you are big enough now to come with us. We know we'll be proud of you."

We know from experience that this kind of preparation *does* work. Children will astound you by how well they respond when they know what is expected of them. (Of course, it helps if you practice good table manners at home.)

Let children know what you expect of them. In the second story, Ken and Lydia had made a common mistake. Both of them led such busy lives, they had fallen into the habit of casual living. Meals were eaten in the kitchen, timetables were lax, arguments were left to work themselves out. Neither of them had stopped to say, "When company comes, and we want to show them that we are glad they came, we make a special effort. We greet them warmly, we put aside books and talk to them and listen. We eat in the dining room, and allow time to put on clean clothes. At the end of the meal, during which *everyone* takes part in the conversation, you wait until everyone is through, then you clear the table and come in and join the rest of us. You show your guests that they are more important than any television program, and when they leave, you let them know you really want them to come again."

Keep expectations reasonable. There are so many times when children are forced into situations without warning or preparation. These ventures into the world can be upsetting for children and embarrassing for their parents, or they can be pleasant for everyone concerned, *if* expectations are reasonable and the children have been prepared in advance.

31

"Do we have to go to school tonight?"

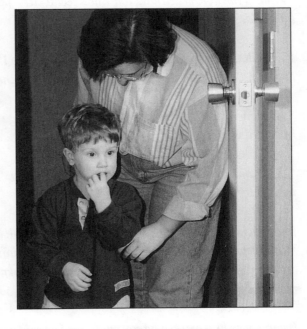

Not listening to children's concerns

"Do we **have** to go to school tonight?" asked three year old Brian unhappily. "Can't we just stay home?"

Dennis Chalmers looked at his son in surprise. "Of course we have to go," he said firmly. "Come on, now, we don't want to be late."

In the car, Dennis and Janet were busy catching up on the news of their respective days, and didn't notice that Brian was being unusually quiet. Once they were inside, it became obvious that something was wrong. This Parents' Night program was meant to show the mothers and fathers what their children had been accomplishing, and most of the kids were eagerly taking their parents around the room, but not Brian. He was clinging to his mother's hand, not breaking away to talk to his friends, and not dragging his parents over to see his art work on the wall.

"What's the matter, Brian, don't you feel well?" Janet asked quietly, drawing him aside? "You seem very unhappy."

He hesitated, then looked up anxiously. "Why do I have to change teachers? I like Ms. DeAngelis. I don't want to move to another room."

"Whatever gave you the idea that you had to change teachers?" asked his father in astonishment.

"You came to school with me," said Brian simply. "Whenever you come with me, I have to go to a new teacher."

Janet looked at Dennis. "It's true," she said. "We haven't been to a Parents' Night before, but we've been here twice when Brian changed rooms. It hadn't occurred to me." She turned to their son. "It's okay, honey, we just came to visit tonight," she said. "Ms. DeAngelis is still your teacher."

Brian's face broke into a happy smile, and he said eagerly, "Come see the block tower I made."

Be alert for atypical behavior

Dennis and Janet missed their cue when Brian first expressed his anxiety. This was not typical behavior for their son, and it should have alerted them to the fact that something was not quite right. If they had asked a few questions then, instead of later, Brian would have been spared the worry and unhappiness he was feeling.

Find out why the child is protesting. Too often adults brush aside their children's protests. Does "I don't feel good. Can I stay home today?" translate in your mind into, is he having problems with school? Or do you check his temperature?

If five year old Holly doesn't want to go on a Sunday afternoon visit to your sister's house, protesting that she doesn't like Kimberly, do you say briskly, "Nonsense, Kimberly is your cousin, of course you like her." Or do you question Holly and find out that seven year old Kimberly has been bossing Holly around, making her do things she didn't want to do and generally making life miserable for her?

If Xavier, in your third grade class, says he didn't hear you when you asked him a question, do you scold him for not paying attention? Or do you observe Xavier for a week, watching for any signs that he has a hearing problem?

How do you know when to ignore a child and when to listen? Perhaps a child *is* trying to get out of something, or avoid punishment, but *perhaps* there's an underlying reason for the protests. How do you know when to ignore and when to listen? You use all you have learned about this child and how he or she functions. If you aren't sure, err on the side of belief and provide a listening ear.

32

"Even grown-ups cry when they get hurt."

Bribes or rewards?

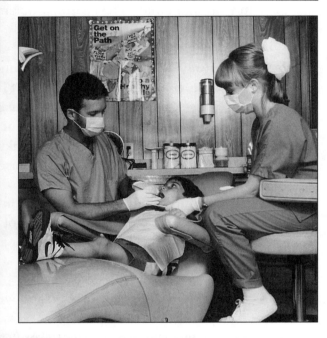

Allen
"I know I'll cry, and mommy will get mad."

"Now listen to me, Allen," said Mrs. Benson sternly. "The last time you went to the dentist, I was ashamed of the way you carried on. You're five years old, not a baby! If you want that new game you've been begging for, you'd better not cry today. But if you're real brave, I'll get it for you on the way home."

Allen's stomach churned and his heart thumped. How can I not cry when it hurts so badly? he wondered miserably. I know I'll cry, and mommy will be mad. She's mean. She's making me get hurt, and I won't ever get the game I want.

Tears were rolling down Allen's cheeks before he even got into the dentist's chair. He sat with muscles tense, and the minute he saw the drill in Dr. Vitucci's hand he started to sob—sobs which turned to screams as soon as the drill touched him.

That was a terrible day for Allen—a day of pain, shame and a feeling of injustice.

Toby
"I'm so proud of you."

"Toby, I know you don't want to go to the dentist today," said Mrs. Lambert. "The last time it hurt so much you couldn't help crying. It's all right. Even grown-ups cry sometimes when they get hurt."

Her five year old son looked at her with a mixture of surprise and gratitude. "I thought you were mad at me," he said.

"No, I wasn't mad at you before, and I won't be mad if it happens again, but I'll tell you a secret. When I was a little girl, I was afraid to go to the dentist, and I screamed till they could hear me a mile away. But when I got older, I realized that I was crying before I ever got hurt. I started yelling the minute I even heard the sound of the drill. So I decided to wait, and not cry until I needed to, and you know what? The hurting time didn't last long at all. It was all over before I knew it.

"If you cry today, don't worry about it. Dr. Jorgenson will be as careful as he can, and I'll be right there."

Toby thought about what his mother had said, and the tears didn't start as soon as he climbed into the chair, the way they had the last time, nor did he cry as loud or as long.

When they left the office, his mother stooped down and gave him a hug. "I'm so proud of you, Toby. You tried so hard—you were very brave. What do you say we stop on the way home and get that new game you've been wanting?"

What is the difference between a bribe and a reward?

Mrs. Benson used bribes and threats. It didn't work, and chances are that every trip Allen made to the dentist after that was more of an ordeal for both of them.

Mrs. Lambert offered reassurance and reason and rewarded Toby for doing the best he could. Toby was undoubtedly more able to deal with dentists and other unpleasant situations as he grew older.

A bribe is something promised in advance if a child does what you want her to. A reward is given after an event, in return for a child's doing his best.

What about the gold stars or seals so often used with older children, as well as the very young? It depends on your approach, how often you give them, and what you hope to achieve. Do you say, "If you finish your math paper, I'll give you a gold star?" Or do you quietly put the star on the finished paper?

Do you give a star for every paper finished? Do you put them on a chart on the wall, so Meg, who is slow at math, sees Emilio's row stretching way beyond hers? If Meg copies someone else's paper when you aren't looking, is it the chart that pushed her into cheating? And how much will those stars mean to Emilio if he doesn't have to make any effort to get them?

What do you want to achieve? Do you want your students to finish papers only because they are concerned about their grade? Or do you want them to learn, to think, to work out answers and to feel proud of what they have accomplished?

Sometimes parents offer their children money for a good report card or for cleaning their room. Does this teach the lesson that you only do your best, or contribute your share, if the payoff is good enough?

Remember, children live up to your expectations. If you *assume* that they will do their best work in school, if you *expect* that they will take pride in their home and do their fair share to keep it a comfortable place, they will probably do what you hope they will. I say "probably," because there is another side to this coin. If you want your children to take the hard way, to exert effort when it is easier to let things slide, you must give them the reward of recognition and appreciation. Not money, but words.

"That's a great report card, Juan. I know how hard you worked to make those B's." "Thanks for helping me clean out the garage, Holly. I know you'd rather have been playing ball, but we got a lot more done together than I could have done alone. I certainly appreciate it."

We all like to be valued when we do our best. When you value children's efforts, everyone reaps the rewards.

Bibliography for Part Three

Books for parents and teachers

Carton, Lonnie. (1992). *"No" Is a Love Word: How to Say "NO" to Children of all Ages Firmly, Fairly, Consistently and Without Guilt.* Boston: Learning Center. This book is available through the Learning Center, PO Box 204, Newton Branch, Boston, MA 02258, 1-617-332-7472.

Cherry, Claire. (1985). *Please Don't Sit on Your Kids: A Parent's Guide to Nonpunitive Discipline.* Carthage, IL: Fearon Teaching Aids.

Essa, Eve. (1983). *Practical Guide to Solving Preschool Behavior Problems.* Albany, NY: Delmar.

Faber, Adele and Mazlich, Elaine. (1982). *How to Talk so Kids Will Listen and Listen so Kids Will Talk.* New York: Avon Books.

Feiden, Karyn L. (1991). *Raising Responsible Kids: Preschool Through the Teen Years.* Englewood Cliffs, NJ: Prentice Hall.

Mitchell, Grace L. (1982). *A Very Practical Guide to Discipline With Young Children.* Glen Burnie, MD: Telshare Publishing Company.

Nordling, Jo A. (1992). *Taking Charge: A Parent and Teacher Guide to Loving Discipline.* San Jose, CA: R & E Publishers, Inc.

Saiffer, Steffen. (1990). *Practical Solutions to Practically Every Problem—The Early Childhood Manual.* St. Paul, MN: Redleaf.

Samalin, Nancy and Whitney, Catherine. (1992). *Love and Anger: The Parental Dilemma*. New York: Penguin Books.

Samalin, Nancy and Jablow, Martha Moraghan. (1988). *Loving Your Child Is Not Enough: Positive Discipline That Works*. New York: Penguin Books.

Afterword

Using the "I Am! I Can!" philosophy

In this book we have frequently referred to the *I Am! I Can!* philosophy. We cannot overemphasize the importance of making that philosophy part of your thinking. When children experience success and feel *I Can!*, that energizes their *I Am!* and leads to future success. When planning for children, **everything** should be measured against one guideline—does it help the child's self-esteem, or weaken it? Will it help **all** the children, or only the ones who are already succeeding? Can you change a game or situation that makes some children winners and others losers? Put the accent on the enjoyment of the games, not competition. For example, if you are having relay races by teams, balance the teams so there are slow runners and fast runners on each team. The slow runners on the winning team can experience the feeling of success that is not often theirs. Being on the losing team will help the fast runners understand what it feels like not to be on top. The slow runners are sharing the responsibility for the loss with the rest of the team, and **all** of them can learn to lose (or win) with grace—and that is important, too.

Acknowledge mistakes in a matter-of-fact way, so the child does not feel shame or embarrassment. "Your kite doesn't fly, Howard? I must have made twenty kites before I made one that flew. Would you like me to go over the directions with you?"

There's a fine line between making everything too easy and pushing too hard. Teachers and parents both **want** to help a children get beyond their stumbling blocks and move ahead. If a child isn't learning, growing and experiencing success, the *I Am* becomes "I don't think I can," or even, "I can't."

Teachers and parents are always learning and growing. Part of the process of growing as adults is opening your mind to new ideas, viewpoints and attitudes.

Recently, we visited a public school in Gauldin, California, where we saw how computers can be used to reinforce the *I Am*. A class of first and second graders were divided into pairs, each pair having a computer in front of them. They were intently watching a teacher at the front of the room and following her directions. On their own monitors they duplicated the patterns she was showing on a big screen, and answered questions about those patterns. They worked as teams, helping each other, solving problems together.

Afterwards, we talked to the director of the whole program. "That was impressive and exciting," we commented, "but we are focusing on discipline. Do you see any connection?"

"Absolutely!" she said firmly. "We have children from every grade level who have been having severe discipline problems in their classrooms. They get caught up in this. Why not? It's like magic to them. And soon they are using the computers successfully. Often it is the first time they have ever succeeded, and you can see the difference. Once they know they **can** do something **well**, their confidence grows, and it carries over into the classroom."

We are not suggesting that every preschool should have computers for the children, but we **are** saying, open your minds to new ideas. Like all teaching tools, it is the way you use them that counts. Whether you are talking about paper and paints, reading games, Cuisenaire rods, science experiments or computers, you must think beyond the skills you are teaching to the ways that particular tool can help children experience success.

All adults are role models and teachers; so we say to all of you, **learn and grow**. Read, go to conferences, join discussion groups, visit other schools, talk to others with the same problems. As you learn about children, what makes them tick and how you can help **them** learn and grow, your problems with discipline will diminish, and you will welcome each new day with joy.

Index

C

discussing child in front of him, 156-157

divorce *see* stepfamilies, blended families

books about, 90-91

child living with father & stepmother, 52-54

child living with mother and stepfather, 46-50, 58-59

effect of on child, 48, 52-54, 59

effect of on wife who becomes single parent, 22

E

environment

safe

outside, for child who is blind, 102

in a school, 70

badges for identification, 70

expectations

adults', of children, 158

children live up to, 158, 209

exploiting the willing child, 134

of parents enrolling child, 141

unreasonable, *see* unreasonable expectations

F

family

blended, 52-53, Chapter 7, 56-62

changes in structure, 19

definition of, 18

meetings, 61

traditions, 61

unit, formerly, 18

Field Day, *see* competition between children

fighting, *see* violence and children

follow-up

after a plan is made, 89

G

goals

for child learning to read, 130

for child with spina bifida, 114

for teachers in specific areas, 114, 121

need for, 23-24

grandparents raising grandchildren

books about, 91

child behind in school, 32-33

child's viewpoint, 27-28

difficulties of, 29-30, 33-35

generation gap, 30

organizations to contact, 92

reasons for, 19, 29, 34-35

support for, 30, 36

viewpoint of grandparents, 29-30, 33-35

guidelines for inclusive education

all children need to misbehave, 143

educate the other children in class, 146

inform parents of resources

developmental pediatrician, 144

Early Intervention, 144

hospital or clinic, 144

public school system, 144

involve teachers in decisions, 104

parents need time to make decisions, 145

teachers need to be willing, 104, 140, 143